"Michael Mercer's *Dancing with Creation* invites you to explore your own thoughts and connect with your own spirituality. The gentle and intelligent sharing of how to deepen your understanding of God follows the dance of the day with acknowledgement of the dark night to the new morning. These beautiful pages provide validating support for a mindful, conscious embrace of life. *Dancing with Creation* offers a profoundly peaceful place to fully rest."

BRENDA KENYON, LCSW, *Director/Administrator, Community Hospice, Brownsburg, IN*

"If you find yourself caught up in anxiety and distraction day by day, you will welcome Michael Mercer's book *Dancing with Creation*. With eloquence as well as practicality, Mercer offers insights and reflections into the traditional Hours of Prayer in the Christian tradition. Each one offers an invitation to enter into the present moment so as to remain mindful of God's presence as we move through each hour of our day. This book is a prescient reminder that all time is God's and that our greatest task is to pause and take part in the greatest dance of all—daily life."

KATHY HENDRICKS, *Author of Opening the Heart: Reflections, Practices and Prayers to Guide Us toward Beauty and Gratitude*

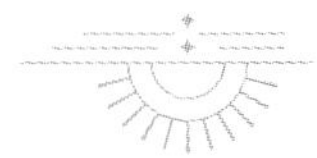

DANCING *with* CREATION

LIVING MINDFULLY THROUGH THE HOURS OF EACH DAY

Michael Mercer

twentythirdpublications.com

Twenty-Third Publications
977 Hartford Turnpike Unit A
Waterford, CT 06385
(860) 437-3012 or (800) 321-0411
twentythirdpublications.com

Photo credits: Unless otherwise indicated, photos are ©Michael Mercer; *cover, page 3*, goami - stock.adobe.com; *page 27*, Smileus - stock.adobe.com; *page 28*, Bobby Stevens Photo - shutterstock.com; *page 61*, bongkarn - stock.adobe.com; *page 88*, Kavita - stock.adobe.com.

ISBN: 978-1-62785-855-7
Printed in the U.S.A.

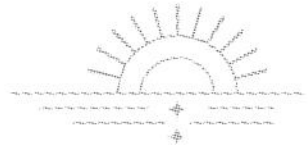

To Gail,
my loving daily companion
for fifty years.

To my children and grandchildren,
I hope for you the daily joys I have known:
music and baseball, interesting books and friends,
good work, travel, and laughter.

In memory of Michael and Denise Spencer,
who gifted me a future beyond evangelicalism and
opened undreamed-of doors of daily vocation for me.

In honor of my colleagues at Community Hospice,
who repair the world a bit every day and advance shalom.

And thank you
to the good people at Gethsemani Abbey
in Trappist, Kentucky

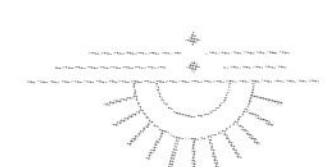

CONTENTS

How to Read This Book

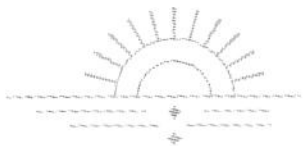

Dancing with Creation uses the structure of the traditional Hours of Prayer in Christian tradition as a template through which we can live each day. The Hours teach us that each day flows and changes with the rhythms of the created world and the life-situations in which we find ourselves.

- The introductory material seeks to help us view each twenty-four-hour day as the focus for our living.
- Then, the book starts in the dark, early morning hours after midnight, when the day begins. It proceeds through early morning, the movement of the normal workday, and ends with evening and bedtime.

You may profitably read this book straight through to get an overall picture of how life moves through each day and night, the themes we often encounter during those movements, and how we can thoughtfully and prayerfully respond to life, God, ourselves, and others.

You may also find benefit in giving attention to certain times of the day when the themes pertaining to those hours find resonance within your own current life seasons and circumstances. For example, if you have trouble sleeping and find yourself combating fears, go to the chapter "Vigils" to read about finding peace in the darkness. Or, if you are in a season of life where you are thinking through work, vocation, or career matters, you might find that concentrating on the chapters on The Little Hours will be helpful.

Each chapter ends with a summary (Remember) and a few questions (Consider) to help you think through and apply what you've read.

I have also tried to sprinkle this book with Scriptures, quotes, poems, and sayings to give you material on which to meditate throughout the course of each day. I believe strongly in the power of imagination to inspire and shape our thinking and living. I hope you will feel free to dip into the book regularly and find imaginative stimulation through engaging these morsels of insight.

At the very end of the book is a final summary and a list of Scriptures organized by the movements of each day. Use this as a handy resource for review and daily meditation.

The Dance of Each Day

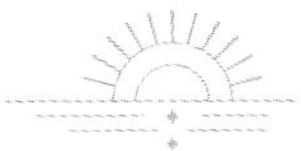

We have but to live, take each day as it comes, see the Lord in all that happens and have a kind of response to the will of God that is much like dancing. You must work with it. It is not a matter of passive submission. This is no way to dance; it is too heavy, too leaden, too dragging and uninspired. No, you must dance with your partner, you must cooperate, you must work with the will of God. This is the sort of dancing that leads to the Kingdom, and makes one free.

FR. MATTHEW KELTY

Quoted by Paul Qenon, OCSO, In Praise of a Useless Life

Overture

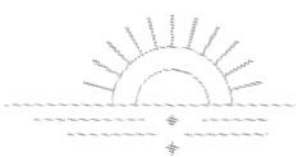

Each day is a gift. I awaken in a world I did not create to play my part in a complex history that has long preceded me, to face people and situations for which I cannot fully plan and over which I have no ultimate control.

Each day is new. Today is not yesterday, nor am I exactly the same person I was yesterday. The hours before me have never been lived before, and I may live into them in ways only constrained by my limited imagination.

Each day is a risk. Wonderful and terrible things may happen, for which I cannot prepare. Am I willing to face this risk?

Each day is a journey. Whether down new roads or on well-worn paths, I walk into a life that is prepared for my awakening and waiting to show me its revelations.

Each day is a mystery. Today will provide clues to follow that can lead me to discover the mundane and extraordinary stuff that holds life together in ways I cannot expect or imagine.

Each day is a puzzle. Moment by moment, I pick up pieces of life and examine them, trying to understand how they fit together and form a coherent picture.

Each day is a story. Or at least a line, paragraph, or chapter. Only by living will it be written. Only by paying attention will it be remembered. Only by remembering will it be told.

Each day is incomplete. Today will not resolve life's questions. At day's end I will not have "arrived." Loose ends and unfinished business will remain. There will be more to do, to learn, to mend. I will still be incomplete and yearning.

Each day is a dance. As the day's rhythms, melodies, and harmonies play and shift, I respond. An unseen Dance Partner shows me the steps and leads. I awkwardly try to follow. The music plays. The dance proceeds.

Prelude

LIVING DAILY

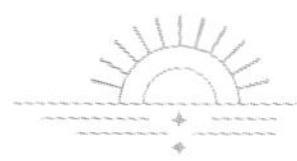

Surely goodness and mercy shall follow me
all the days of my life.

PSALM 23:6

You are the God of my salvation;
for you I wait all day long.

PSALM 25:5

Instructions for living a life:
Pay attention.
Be astonished.
Tell about it.[1]

MARY OLIVER

As a child, I had an illustrated copy of *A Child's Garden of Verses* by Robert Louis Stevenson. I was drawn, delighted, into the world of imagination it created. I grew up in days when we raked up autumn leaves from the grand oaks along the brick-paved street in our small Midwest town, pushed them to the curb and burned them. I can still see the picture in Stevenson's book and feel the acrid smell in my nose.

Sing a song of seasons!
Something bright in all!
Flowers in the summer,
Fires in the fall!

The author had been a sickly child, often confined to bed because of chronic lung issues. What strikes me about this marvelous children's book is how attentive the homebound Stevenson is to the movements of each day and the changing of the seasons. For example, he describes falling asleep at night as the steady march of a military parade or circus that inevitably leads to slumber:

Armies and emperor and kings,
All carrying different kinds of things,
And marching in so grand a way,
You never saw the like by day.

...As first they move a little slow,
But still the faster on they go,

And still beside me close I keep
Until we reach the town of Sleep.

By day, the swing in his yard becomes a ship with pirate adventures. The wind in the trees at night is a man galloping by on horseback, and the stars reflected on the wall "keep going round" in his head. Elevated on pillow hills, he becomes a giant who oversees "The Land of Counterpane," where his toys inhabit an entire country.

The boy observes his shadow, a constant companion that goes "in and out" with him and has a funny habit of changing over the hours. He asks the reader, "What are you able to build with your blocks?"—a question that provoked my imagination—and then describes the "town by the sea" he created.

Yet as I saw it, I see it again,
The kirk and the palace, the ships and the men,
And as long as I live and where'er I may be,
I'll always remember my town by the sea.

At night he journeys to "The Land of Nod."

All by myself I have to go,
With none to tell me what to do—
All alone beside the streams
And up the mountain-sides of dreams.

Day and night. While he was confined to his bed, his imagination thrived. Despite the limited nature of his world, a young boy's fancy soars. Each day is an adventure of discovery and play. No wonder Stevenson's collection was among the most influential children's books of the nineteenth century. With delight, he affirms:

The world is so full of a number of things,
I'm sure we should all be as happy as kings.

Like Stevenson, I extend an invitation for us to live daily—to embrace the wondrous discoveries to be found in the stuff of each day. Like the boy in *A Child's Garden of Verses*, I encourage us to closely observe each day's movements and features. To pay attention to today. To focus on these lived hours, receiving them as a gift to be unwrapped and savored. To concentrate on the day, each twenty-four-hour period, as a distinct unit of time with all its varied aspects, responding to the rhythms and themes it brings.

To live mindfully each day.

For this, we will need focus and imagination.

Life today does not always encourage this. Our technologically immersed culture flattens the world into what is happening on our screens. Distracted, we miss subtle changes in the day around us. Preoccupied in virtual reality, we can't mindfully engage the life before us. We're in danger of losing what it means to be day-to-day-life–shaped people. Bigger forces manipulate our thoughts, feelings, and opinions. In the light of our screens we become passive, influenced by algorithms that greedily demand our attention.

Technology has always given us tools that modify human behavior. Whether print media, radio, movies, television, the ways we've consumed music over the years, or the internet, social media, and AI, tech advances change the way we access and interact with the world, altering human consciousness, behavior, and relationships. I'd argue that the latest technologies have potential to alter our lives as never before.

In *The Anxious Generation*, Jonathan Haidt raises alarms about what tech does to young people, charging that they are "test subjects for a radical new way of growing up, far from the real-world interactions of small communities in which humans evolved." He calls it "the Great Rewiring of Childhood."

Two significant shifts have contributed to this rewiring. First, incessant exposure to screens, especially with ever-available smartphones. Also, "the well-intentioned and disastrous shift toward overprotecting children and restricting their autonomy in the real world." Haidt laments the loss of "free play," where children are given liberty to explore and discover the world for themselves. In other words, because we are overprotecting children from experiencing life in the real world and underprotecting them from indulging in the virtual world, we are producing an "anxious generation" with growing mental health issues and a reduced capacity to flourish as fully formed human beings.

> ...the most rapid rewiring of human relationships and consciousness in human history has made it harder for all of us to think, focus, forget ourselves enough to care about others, and build close relationships.[2]

This is not just a problem for children. I sit next to parents and grandparents on the sidelines of soccer fields who scroll through TikTok videos while ignoring their own kids playing in front of them. I find myself with family members, friends, or strangers, all sitting with heads down, staring at screens, drawn into virtual worlds. I have engaged in long, fruitless arguments on social media. I've caught myself doomscrolling or chasing links for hours, my mind trapped by vacuous stimulation. Anyone can easily spend hours a day lost in galaxies far, far away from real life.

In her book *Alone Together*, Sherry Turkle expresses concern that "technology makes us forget what we know about life."[3] When we replace personal encounters with virtual ones, avoiding messy face-to-face interactions with other people, our capacity for empathy decreases. We miss the insights we gain about ourselves and others from intimate engagement. She questions if we have calculated the balance between what we've gained and what we've lost in accessing the world virtually.

> *...the spirit is not strong enough because it is continually being dissipated in restless, undisciplined activity.*[4]
>
> **PIERRE TEILHARD DE CHARDIN**

Techno-diversion is only the latest, most potent example of how humans get distracted from living daily. It has always been a struggle to live mindfully. So, this is not a book primarily about disconnecting from tech. The problem goes beyond screen distraction. We battle whatever steals our attention.

This book is for me first. I recognize my own need to put away distractions and refocus my own heart on living through each day's hours with due regard, thoughtfully and prayerfully. I can get distracted by anything, and frequently am. Our days are too few to miss out on what they offer us:

- The rhythms of life to which I may respond
- The people I meet with whom I may thoughtfully interact
- The daily work I can do to repair the world, if even just a little
- Opportunities to find rest, refreshment, and pure enjoyment in being alive
- The subtle signs all around me that suggest I'm living in a God-soaked world
- The mystery of human experience to discover: so rich, so terrible, so curious
- The dance that creation calls me to, which I may join—awkward though my steps may be

A key attitude in daily living is responsiveness. We plan and live responsibly, yes, but without preconceived notions. We remain open to listening, watching, and exploring what the day is bringing us, not what we impose upon the day. We accept that there will always be more to discover and respond to, and that we will probably miss more than we catch.

Every day is made up of distinct periods of time, each with its own rhythms and themes. A day is not a static entity but a dynamic space in which life is flowing and adapting. Morning has a different feel than late afternoon. Night is a world of its own. And so on. Each day calls us to mind these movements, to respond to the flow and where it might take us. Each day invites us to dance!

Devotees in all major religions have known this and followed practices to mark each day's movements. In Christian tradition, days are divided into set hours of prayer, called the "Divine Hours." Christians stayed true to their Jewish roots and later assimilated patterns of Roman society for organizing each day. I have found the divisions they mark a helpful way to think through the various movements and themes of days and nights. Some even say these Hours are God's angels, calling us to live mindfully.

> The hours are the seasons of the day, and they were originally understood in a mythical way. Earlier generations of our human race, not ruled by alarm clocks, saw the hours personified, encountered them as messengers of eternity in the natural flow of time growing, blossoming, bearing fruit. In the unfolding rhythm of everything that grows and changes on earth each hour had a character and presence infinitely richer and more complex than our sterile clock time. As messenger from another dimension—an angel as it were—each

hour was understood to have its own significance.[5]

■ DAVID STEINDL-RAST AND SHARON LEBELL

What a beautiful thought! Angels sent to get our attention and lead us! Their messages encourage us to sense the day's movements and respond with deepened awareness. I'm no angel, but I'd like to join them in calling us to join each day's dance.

A "Book of Hours" is a resource that helps people meditate and pray at designated times through the day. Here's how Fr. Pierre Teilhard de Chardin's Book of Hours describes the day's divisions:

> Each "hour" (Dawn, Day, Dusk, and Dark) evokes a specific mood to support us as we transition through our days on Earth. For example, the Dawn hour welcomes the day, and the prayers are an invitation to greater wakefulness and praise. The Day hour is focused on work, challenging us with exhortations and examens, propelling us on throughout our tasks. The Dusk hour is a chance to reflect on the lived day, offering gratitude and peaceful transition into the evening. Lastly, the Dark hour is meditative, to lull us into the close of the day and feed our dreams.[6]

So, shall we dance? I invite you to join me in responding to the rhythms of each day. As we try to move in sync with them, may we learn to live more mindfully, for our sake and for the life of the world.

Come, let us dance each day with creation!

Remember...

Each day is made up of distinct periods of time, each with its own rhythms and themes. Living daily involves giving mindful attention to how each day flows and changes.

Many things distract us and make it hard to pay attention throughout the course of each day. This is especially true in our current technologically oriented world.

Living daily means to view each day dynamically and to respond to its movements.

Consider...

What would you say is your approach to each day?

What things distract you from paying attention to life around you and in you as you go through each day?

How do you balance taking initiative and exercising control with being open and responsive?

SOURCES

1. Oliver, Mary. "Sometimes," from *Devotions*. New York: Penguin Press, 2017.

2. Haidt, Jonathan. *The Anxious Generation: How the Great Rewiring of Childhood Is Causing an Epidemic of Mental Illness*. Penguin Publishing Group, Kindle Edition, 2024.

3. Turkle, Sherry. *Alone Together: Why We Expect More from Technology and Less from Each Other*. Basic Books, Kindle Edition, 2017.

4. Deignan, Kathleen, CND; Osgood, Libby, CND. *Teilhard de Chardin: A Book of Hours*. Orbis Books, Kindle Edition, 2023.

5. Steindl-Rast, Brother David; Lebell, Sharon. *Music of Silence: A Sacred Journey through the Hours of the Day*. Ulysses Press, Kindle Edition, 2001.

6. Deignan, Kathleen, CND; Osgood, Libby, CND.

Sinfonia

RENEWING A VISION OF DAILY LIFE WITHIN CREATION

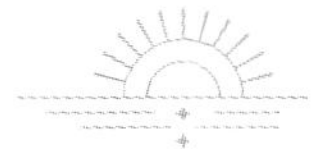

Day to day pours forth speech,
and night to night declares knowledge.

PSALM 19:2

By day the Lord commands his steadfast love,
and at night his song is with me,
a prayer to the God of my life.

PSALM 42:8

Light is constant, we just turn over in it.[1]

MARILYNNE ROBINSON

A good creation of possibility and peril

Living in this world through each day and night is a dance we do with creation, as the world turns light to dark and back to light again. We step in relation to the light, moving toward or away from it. Basking in its warm embrace or reaching for dawn, we turn, turn, turn through the rhythms of creation's days and nights. It is how God made the world and how God made us to live.

When we listen to these turnings and step to the rhythms of light and darkness, we discover the goodness and possibilities of a world in which we can order our lives. To use imagery from the creation story:

- When we join the dance, we overcome the chaos of a disordered, unfilled life.
- We distinguish light from darkness and find that we can dance with them both.
- We separate and name those elements that give our life structure and balance.
- We taste the blessed, abundant life intended for us.
- We enter God's world and join God in filling it with life that flourishes.
- And it is very good.

The Bible describes creation in a pattern of seven days during which the Creator speaks and acts. Genesis 1 is a poetic liturgy written to help us imagine this world's goodness and fecundity. God gives the world, at first described as "formless and empty," structure and fills it with burgeoning life and blessing.

This Creation Liturgy was first spoken to Jewish exiles in Babylon, whose lives were in chaos. They had lost their homes, land, temple, and nation—all that was familiar and meaningful to them. In exile, they sought to reestablish their identity as people blessed by God. These words came to them as good news, proclaiming that their God could overcome chaos! God, unlike the Babylonian gods, could do what had been done in the beginning—turn chaos into something orderly, purposeful, and life-enhancing.

In Christian tradition, the creation account has been taught as describing a perfect original world, a pristine ecosystem without sin, evil, or death—a paradise long ago that humans subsequently lost. That is not, however, the world of Genesis 1. Dark chaos was present from the beginning, and creation needed care lest it return to chaos, so God made humans to nurture and protect it. Those who put the Creation Liturgy at the beginning of the Bible did so because an account of God taming chaos and providing abundant life was just the word of hope the Jewish exiles needed. As Walter Brueggemann says:

> The text is likely dated to the sixth century B.C. and addressed to exiles. It served as a refutation of Babylonian theological claims. The Babylonian gods seemed to control the future. They had, it appeared, defeated the dreams of the God of Israel. Against such claims, it is here asserted that Yahweh is still God, one who watches over his creation and will bring it to well-being.... To despairing exiles, it is declared that the God of Israel is the Lord of all of life.[2]

The Creation Liturgy introduces us to the world as the ancient Israelites knew it, the world God made, the world as it is and has always been—a "good" but not "perfect" world, a world of great potential that God organized out of chaos so that life could emerge and be sustained. Not a paradise since lost, but the same fertile world of possibility and peril humans have always known.

Humans are God's stewards to protect and care for this world so that God's blessing might fill it. Like the exiles, we put our hope in the Creator and rejoice in God's ability to tame chaos and enhance life. Genesis 1 is good news for us all. This same world of possibility and peril is God's gift to us all. God calls us to live daily in it, with gratitude, mindful of its well-being.

That's right! Today, God calls you and me to join the dance held each day and night in this good creation. The Creator, who is always making things new, invites us to rise above chaos, discover the rhythms of God's creative acts, and move within those rhythms for our own blessing and to bless others.

And for all this, nature is never spent;
There lives the dearest freshness deep down things;
And though the last lights off the black West went
Oh, morning, at the brown brink eastward, springs —
Because the Holy Ghost over the bent
World broods with warm breast and with ah! bright wings.[3]

GERARD MANLEY HOPKINS

Renewing my vision of creation

When I, like the ancient Hebrews, need to refresh this vision of creation and daily life in my heart, I have found a place to do that. I travel south and spend time in retreat among the Trappist monks at the Abbey of Gethsemani in the Knob Region of north-central Kentucky. Gethsemani is best known as the Abbey where monk and author Thomas Merton served and is now buried.

I was fifty-five years old when I made my initial visit to Gethsemani. The place exudes a tangible silence. I found myself in awe. Unlike Merton, I did not go there to become a Trappist. I had been a pastor in mostly low-church, evangelical congregations—as far from monasteries, monks' vows, and silence as one could get. However, through unforeseen circumstances, my pastoring life ended and I found myself lost. A journey to Gethsemani was part of finding my way again.

At that time I was lead writer for the Internet Monk blog, founded by my late friend Michael Spencer. He bequeathed that honor to me, and I'm forever grateful. A few friends and I carried on the conversation at Internet Monk for ten years after Michael's death. A Baptist, Spencer called his blog *Internet Monk* because he had grown to admire the well-known and somewhat infamous monk Thomas Merton. Merton's earthy persona and spiritual authenticity were profoundly attractive to Michael, and the monk's writings became for him a door to the broader history, tradition, and practices of the Church.

Here's how Michael described him:

> Tom Merton made an unforgettable impression on everyone who met him. No one ever nominated him for perfection. He could be selfish, manipulative and vain, often putting his friends through absurd abuses to get him out of the monastery and into the city. He gossiped, and often whined. He seldom paused to be content, and often enjoyed being an irritant. He sometimes drank too much and could hold a grudge for years. Yet, the unanimous verdict of those who knew him in life and those who know him through his voluminous literary output is that Merton was an authentic human being of the rarest sort and master of the things of the spirit. Words like genuine, self-knowledgeable and deeply

> spiritual occur again and again in descriptions of Merton. People sought him out from all over the world because of what they sensed in his writing.[4]

Spencer's passion for this modern monk piqued my interest, so I began to read Merton and then made my own pilgrimage to Gethsemani. Driving south from Indiana, I exited into the "Bourbon Trail" region of Kentucky, cruised through quaint Bardstown, and then wound my way through the wooded countryside toward Abraham Lincoln's birthplace. Soon I reached the Abbey.

In 1848, Cistercian monks of the Strict Observance (Trappists) from Melleray Abbey in France came to Kentucky. Gethsemani was the first Abbey they established in the United States. Trappists follow the Rule of St. Benedict, ordering life around daily rhythms of prayer, reading, and manual labor in an atmosphere of silent contemplation. As they say: "Each activity enriches the other, keeping our hands, hearts and minds fully alive—so that we are always ready to listen and respond to God's call."[5]

Upon arrival, I was welcomed and given directions to my room in the Monastery Wing just off the balcony of the church. I climbed the stone stairs, unlocked the door of my room, and found the following instructions for retreatants on the desk:

> **The Gethsemani Silent Retreat**
>
> *A retreat here at the Abbey is meant to provide two important things:*
>
> 1. A sharing in the monastic liturgy.
> 2. The elements of silence and solitude, so as to be open to God in a particular way that is not always available in the world today.

My room was plain—bed, chair and desk, an icon and crucifix on the wall. The dining room downstairs and other public spaces, designated for silence, were spare and pleasant, with large windows looking out on well-kept grounds, a winding walkway past the Stations of the Cross, and busy bird feeders. We ate simple, nourishing meals, with added treats of homemade fudge, a delicious product of the monks' labors.

As for the Abbey Church itself, Merton deemed it a fine example of Cistercian architecture, marked by simplicity and energy, encouraging humility and prayer. It is indeed austere, but its soaring interior space, the delightful, ever-shifting patterns of light streaming through stained glass windows, and the profound silence absorbed into the sanctuary walls combine to promote awe, contemplation, and prayerfulness.

During my stay, I kept mainly to the church, the silent areas, and the grounds outside. To the southwest is Cross Knob, where you ascend a mound to a large stone cross that keeps watch over farmland, woods, lakes, and knobs surrounding the Abbey. There are nearly 1,500 acres of land with trails, some of which take you to spots where you may contemplate statuary or pray at small shrines.

Once I had surveyed the place, I went back to my room and in the silence I slept, as Elijah did after his long escape into the desert (1 Kings 19). Little did I realize how exhausted I was from my work and grief. I fell hard into the quiet and slept long, awakening with a deep sense of rest.

Then I breathed. I ate. I walked. I took pictures. I read. And I participated in the Hours of prayer.

The monks pray the Divine Hours each day. Following this ancient Church tradition, their prayers break the silence seven times a day when they gather in choir to chant the psalms.

My initial retreat at Gethsemani was the first time I became fully aware of this traditional practice. It was not part of my background. But praying the psalms at fixed hours has always been integral to the Church's life, an inheritance from her Jewish roots: "Seven times a day I praise you" (Psalm 119:164). The New Testament likewise portrays Jesus and the apostles praying at set hours.

When Christians scattered across the Roman Empire, they adapted their prayer times to the daily patterns of local life. The Romans rang bells at various hours to organize the conduct of each business day, and these became the hours when Christians prayed. Later, St. Benedict adapted these patterns and designed the template that has informed the practice of fixed-hour prayer throughout Church history.

This was all new to me. My devotional practices had been formed in a different spiritual milieu. Ordering life around liturgical prayers was unheard of. But in the Hours I found a rhythm which gave structure to the day and spoke peace. The seven Hours of prayer became to me something like the seven days of creation were to the Jewish exiles—an orderly pattern of good news, blessing, and purpose. I felt I was joining the dance of creation as I marked the turning of each day around the light, relishing its goodness.

The seven fixed Hours of prayer are as follows (with their Latin names):

- Vigils (night)
- Lauds (dawn)
- Terce (morning)
- Sext (noon)
- None (mid-afternoon)
- Vespers (evening)
- Compline (end of day)

Each community is free to adapt the specific times for these prayers. Some omit the "Little Hours" of Terce, Sext, and None, gathering only for morning, noon, and evening prayers. If one divides the day evenly, Vigils falls at 3:00 a.m. and the other Hours follow at three-hour intervals: 6:00 a.m., 9:00 a.m., 12 noon, 3:00 p.m., 6:00 p.m., 9:00 p.m. The Hours at Gethsemani were adjusted to suit their particular schedule.

Fixed-hour prayer is unique in that it represents continual prayer. As Father Timothy Gallagher says:

> The Liturgy of the Hours differs, however, from other liturgical prayer precisely as a prayer *of the hours*. The Mass, for example, though unparalleled in its spiritual richness, is celebrated at one moment in the day; the Liturgy of the Hours provides liturgical prayer throughout the entire day: morning, midday, evening, and night. It is the Church's greatest gift to hearts that long for prayerful communion with God throughout the day.[6]

At Gethsemani, cued by bells and accompanied by organ, each Hour begins with a petition for God's presence and help, followed by a psalm and hymn of invitation. Then two or three psalms are chanted. The monks sit on both sides of the sanctuary, facing each other and chanting responsively, or responding to cantors who stand in the aisle between them. The congregation is encouraged to participate. The psalms are followed by readings, responses, prayers, the Commemoration of Our Lady, and a dismissal. After each element, a doxology is sung:

Praise the Father, the Son and Holy Spirit,
both now and forever,
the God who is, who was, and is to come,
at the end of the ages.

The spirit of these prayer times is sweet; the chanting melodic, unpretentious, and reverent. The services are brief, fifteen minutes or so, providing oases of rest and perspective in the midst of daily activities.

Living, not just praying the Hours

As much as I appreciated the blessing of praying with the monks while on retreat, I did not come home from Gethsemani determined to take up praying the Hours daily. However, the Hours made me realize something fundamental about how each day flows. They mark each day's shifting "music" and changing themes. Beyond the practice itself, I saw I could try to pattern my life after what those Hours represent.

Vigils (*night prayer*) encourages me to contemplate the role of darkness and night in my life. It prompts me to face my fears, trust God as my refuge, and learn the benefits of darkness.

Lauds (*morning prayer*) awakens me to the dawn and the gift and promise of each new day. It speaks of new hope, possibilities, wonders waiting to be discovered and shared with others.

Terce (*beginning of workday*) reminds me to reflect upon my vocation, the various callings in my life, and how I might go about my work this day.

Sext (*midday*) reminds me to work well and to watch for tests that try to throw me off track. It encourages me to trust God to help, save, comfort, and defend me throughout the day.

None (*end of workday*), near the completion of my daily labors, encourages me to finish the day well and begin reflecting on my work, as God did at the close of each creation day.

Vespers (*evening*) provides time to reflect and give thanks. In the slower evening hours, I can find refreshment, peace, and renewal at the end of the day.

Compline (*close of day*) bids me enter the Great Silence (the time of sleep) in a spirit of childlike trust, placing the coming night, my life, and my future under God's loving protection and care.

This pattern of the Hours is a metaphor to help us live mindfully, to walk with God in the rhythms of daily life. I hope paying attention to the themes these divisions suggest will guide us, as the seven-day pattern of creation guided the Jewish exiles, into a renewed sense of identity, hope, and purpose. I will fill this seven-fold form with stories, quotes, and reflections to help us hear the "music" of each day.

May we find it to be "very good." For our own peace and well-being. For the life of the world.

There must be a time
when the man of prayer goes to pray
as if it were the first time in his life
he had ever prayed;
when the man of resolutions puts his
resolutions aside

as if they had all been broken,
and he learns a different wisdom.
Distinguishing the sun from the moon,
the stars from the darkness,
the sea from the dry land,
and the night sky from the shoulder of a hill.[7]

THOMAS MERTON

Remember...

The creation liturgy in Genesis 1 was written as good news to the Jewish exiles in Babylon. It assured them that God could bring order, blessing, and fruitfulness to the chaos of their lives.

We live in the same good, ordered world God created, described in Genesis 1. It is a world of great potential, but also of peril, and we humans are here to attend to its well-being each day.

Using the ancient traditional form of the Divine Hours, we can pay attention to the rhythms and themes of each day in order that we might move and respond to the day's various movements.

Consider...

What chaos would you like God to tame and bring order to in your life?

Have you ever taken a retreat that enriched you and helped you view yourself and life differently? What was it like, and how did it change you?

What, if any, is your understanding and experience of fixed-hour prayers?

SOURCES

1. Robinson, Marilynne. *The Gilead Novels* (Oprah's Book Club). Farrar, Straus and Giroux, Kindle Edition, 2004.

2. Brueggemann, Walter. *Genesis: Interpretation: A Bible Commentary for Teaching and Preaching*. Westminster John Knox Press, 1986.

3. Hopkins, Gerald Manley. "God's Grandeur" (poetryfoundation.org/poems/44395/gods-grandeur).

4. Spencer, Michael. "The Monk Who Wouldn't Go Away" (imonk.blog/2011/01/31/the-monk-who-wouldnt-go-away).

5. www.trappists.org/trappist-life/

6. Gallagher, Timothy, OMV. *Praying the Liturgy of the Hours*. The Crossroad Publishing Company, 2014.

7. Merton, Thomas. *No Man Is an Island*. Harcourt Brace Jovanovich, 1955/1983.

Vigils

FINDING PEACE IN THE DARKNESS

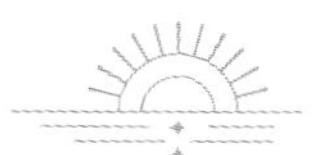

I will give you the treasures of darkness
and riches hidden in secret places...

ISAIAH 45:3

I think of you on my bed,
and meditate on you in the watches of the night...

PSALM 63:6

I need darkness as much as I need light.[1]

BARBARA BROWN TAYLOR

Day begins at night

The Reverend John Ames loved to walk the quiet streets of Gilead, Iowa, in the dark of night. Some nights he couldn't sleep at all and didn't feel like reading, so at one or two in the morning he would "walk down every single street, past every house, in about an hour." The good pastor would think about the people who lived in the houses he passed and pray for them, for peace in the midst of whatever troubled them. As he walked, he noticed that even the trees sounded different at night, and smelled different too. At the end of his walk, he would end up at the church, pray some more, and wait for dawn.

On other nights he was moved to read late—until about three or four in the morning—then take a briefer walk directly to the church, where he watched for morning to come. He loved the "obliging, accommodating" sounds of the church at night, all settled into itself, and entertained the idea that he liked the building even better when it was empty of people.

Then, as if to reward his night vigils, the dawn came.

> So often I have seen the dawn come and the light flood over the land and everything turn radiant at once, that word "good" so profoundly affirmed in my soul that I am amazed I should be allowed to witness such a thing.[2]

Rev. John Ames, the pastoral center and narrator of Marilynne Robinson's luminous novel *Gilead*, knew that nighttime holds treasures for those who will attend to them as they await a new day.

Living daily, we recognize that each day begins in the dark of night. When the clock strikes midnight, the page turns. As Genesis tells it, there was evening and morning, a new day. Long before sunlight, the day is already here, enveloped in darkness. Night prepares the world for day.

This is the grace of God. While most of us sleep, a world prepares itself for our awakening.

Humans live in a twenty-four-hour day-night pattern called circadian rhythms. Experts tell us we evolved to sleep at night as a means of recharging for daytime activities. Sleep provides a number of benefits, including:

- consolidating our memories and helping our brains organize information,
- regulating our emotions and helping us manage stress,
- enhancing our judgment, decision-making, and problem solving,
- conserving our energy and promoting physical immunity, healing, and well-being.

The pattern of sleeping through the night in one long stretch may, however, be a relatively modern invention. In earlier human history, sleep may have been biphasic: that is, it occurred in two distinct phases, not one. This intriguing article summarizes some of what has been learned:

> This is how it happened. As night approached and after a day of extenuating work, people took their first sleep around 9 p.m. After four good hours of sleep, they would wake up around one to carry out some more activities. Naturally, the exact time of sleeping and awakening was relative since there were no alarm clocks; it just happened naturally. To the period right after the first sleep, people gave the name 'the watch.'
>
> The watch was the perfect time to carry out some activities. For religious people that meant praying.... Aside from religious activities, for common people the

> watch was the perfect moment to carry out common tasks like adding more wood to the fire, going to take a leak, feeding their farm animals, doing some household work, mending some clothes, and so on.
>
> ...people also found this gap in the day for socializing and carrying out more intimate activities....As a matter of fact, doctors recommended having intercourse during the watch to conceive, since both would be more relaxed after a good rest....But this time was also used by families to connect and simply talk about basically anything without the pressure of work.
>
> After some good couple hours of well-spent time, people would go back to sleep until dawn or a bit later. This second sleep shift was simply known as morning sleep.[3]

It seems that our ancestors found meaningful activity, connection, and purpose in the middle of the night, making use of the dark hours for more than sleep.

As a hospice chaplain, my sleep was often interrupted when I was called out to work. I know about first and second sleep personally—not because it's natural to me but because people sometimes need my services in the middle of the night.

Once, around midnight, the on-call nurse phoned. A family was requesting my support. She was on her way to attend to a dying patient, family had gathered, and they would like the chaplain to come too.

The dying woman had known a life of distress and dysfunction. Married to an unreliable man, she found herself as a young woman far from where she had grown up, mostly alone, with four little girls to care for. When he left for good, she had a breakdown. The girls went into care and eventually got separated out into foster homes, bereft of mother and each other. The girls found ways to keep in touch over the years, and as adults they had occasionally reconnected. Now they had gathered to keep vigil at Mom's bedside.

Mom had found a measure of healing from her chaotic younger life. She married again, this time to a jewel of a guy, a veteran with a thousand stories, a mischievous smile, and a caring heart. The daughters felt like they'd come home to a complete family.

The nurse confirmed that the patient was actively dying and could pass soon. It took hours, so she and I joined the overnight family vigil. We sat in the dim living room, TV light flickering. We talked, encouraged rest, and quietly sat while family members tried to sleep. Daughters stumbled into the room in pajamas, rubbing eyes and leaning close to say something to mom, then retreated to the sofa or their beds.

There was coffee brewing and snacks, silences and questions. Always there were stories, laughter and tears, reflections on mom and the relationships they had loved, lost, and found again. Some said they didn't know what to think or how to feel. Mostly, we just sat together quietly in the semi-darkness, listening to the shallow, changing breath sounds of the woman in the bed. The night vigil.

The night was peaceful, intimate, thoughtful, profound. Even through these hours of darkness, it felt as though we were waiting for a new life to be born. Hope infused the sadness.

Where does your imagination go when you think of nighttime and darkness? What feelings are evoked when you imagine what happens in the black "wee hours" between midnight and dawn? What do you envision hides in the deep shadows that shroud the world at night?

Light and darkness, good and evil, creatures of the night

I recently read the fascinating book *Night Magic* by Leigh Ann Henion, which chronicles her attempt to embrace and learn from the nighttime hours.

> This is the story of how I set out to re-center darkness by spending time with some of the diverse and awe-inspiring life-forms that are nurtured by it.[4]

Henion details epiphanous encounters with "marvels of the dark." She attends synchronous firefly gatherings, witnesses salamanders emerging from their dark, "under a rock" existence to breed in ephemeral pools, and searches out screech owls and glowworms. A world of night creatures opens up to her at a "Mothapalooza" festival, and she discovers that night is a time of abundance, not scarcity. Putting aside her own aversion, she attempts to become "bat-positive" at a "Bat Blitz" event. She delights in previously unrecognized primroses and other nocturnal-blooming plants all around her.

Henion poignantly observes our ill-considered biases against darkness. Night is "unmapped territory" for most of us. We've forgotten how to see in it and relate to it. We are scarcely aware of the plants and creatures that work the "night shift" to keep this world alive and flourishing. However, she reminds us, it's of invaluable worth. "Darkness is, arguably, the genesis of life itself."[5]

This may prove a hard sell. We've been taught to "make hay while the sun shines" and therefore view night as unproductive "downtime." We use "light" and "dark" as metaphors for good and bad things in life, and the overwhelming verdict is that light is good, dark is bad. Light represents all that is beneficent in the world, whereas darkness stands for evil and fearsome things waiting to attack us. It's difficult to see darkness as anything other than that which threatens well-being. Light delights us. Darkness haunts us.

- We call ignorance and superstition intellectual darkness.
- We conceive of the dark as evil's lair, where the proverbial "monsters beneath our bed" hide.
- We fear the malady of blindness most, because we dread being sentenced to a life in the dark.
- We talk about "dark times" in our lives, when troubles prevail.
- We describe discouragement, depression, and despair as "dark places" to be.
- Movies, TV shows, and books are called "dark" when they uncover life's unseemly underbelly of dysfunction, dissipation, and malevolence.
- Throughout history, dark-skinned people have been considered cursed, and thus have been demonized, considered subhuman, enslaved, and brutalized.

As an example, Henion notes the universal fear and negative appraisal of bats. She notes their (misunderstood) associations with Halloween and blood-sucking vampires, their swooping get-entangled-in-your-hair "attacks" (nothing to do with animus against humans), and the aversion their fierce-looking portraits provoke (captured when bats are in distress). Recently, a worldwide pandemic stoked fears of deadly viruses spreading from bats to humans.

Bats scare us. We avoid them, mark them as evil. Yet, bats are essential "night workers," providing pest control that saves agricultural industries billions of dollars each year, pollination for a variety of important food-producing plants, and seed dispersal that promotes new plant and tree growth. Still, we fear bats with the same vividness as Tolkien imagined Sauron, dark villain of Middle-earth: "black against the pall of cloud, there rose a huge shape of shadow, impenetrable, lightning-crowned, filling all the sky."[6] Darkness—embodied in creatures like bats—horrifies us.

Dark seasons in our lives

We also use the metaphor of darkness to describe trying stretches in our lives. I have been through "dark" times. That's how I perceive them, while the "good" times seem to me full of light, warmth, and comfort.

My mid-life years were particularly dim, foggy, and fearful for me. I was "in the dark" most of the time. I struggled to know how to do my work as a pastor of a small church in crisis. I had no clue how to parent our teenaged children through that challenging time in their lives, especially in the spotlight of moral, cultural, and religious expectations. I felt my own faith changing. I didn't know how to express my doubts about the accepted teachings and practices of our tradition. I wasn't sure where I belonged anymore. Financial stresses assailed us. I had no other prospects. I didn't know how or whom to ask for help.

Leonard Cohen wrote of wandering by dark rivers as though he was in Babylon, among the exiles far from home, not knowing who was lurking in the darkness, hunting him. That was how I felt.

Recently, I watched a "dark" TV show called *The Responder*, about police working nights on gritty streets in Liverpool. Its night scenes are almost unbearably dark as Detective Chris Carson, battling his own inner chaos, gets entangled in relentless cycles of moral and criminal murkiness. He applies for the day shift to try and save his family, but days never pan out. He can't escape the clutches of the night.

In one storyline, Chris confronts a man with dementia standing on a dark street in front of closed shop. The man looks up and asks, "Where's the sun gone?" No matter how Chris tries to redirect him, he asks it over and over again, reinforcing the central questions Chris himself is asking: "Why does the darkness prevail? Why can't I find the light again? Where has it gone?"

With its opaque uncertainty, darkness works against hope. It breeds doubts and instills fear that we'll never see the light again. It can evoke our most existential fear of darkness: death itself.

Let me alone, that I may find a little comfort
before I go, never to return,
to the land of gloom and deep darkness,
the land of gloom and chaos,
where light is like darkness.

JOB 10:20–22

Darkness and Faith

Persons of faith who love and trust God speak of spiritual darkness. Not the darkness of unbelief, but their *faith* experience of being unable to find God in the shadows. This has been called the "dark night of the soul," a term coined by a sixteenth-century Spanish priest named St. John of the Cross. As a modern saint described it:

I am told God loves me—and yet the reality of darkness and coldness and emptiness is so great that nothing touches my soul.[7]

ST. TERESA OF CALCUTTA

The "dark night of the soul" describes what it's like when even the most faithful believer feels spiritually lost and alone, unable to find the enlightening, reassuring guidance of a loving God.

Mother Teresa, cited above, knew years of spiritual gloom with little respite. She came to terms with this by accepting her bleak path as a way to identify with Christ crucified in darkness on the cross. She clung to the hope that darkness can be redemptive, that embracing darkness and abandonment may bring light to others. That out of death's darkness can spring resurrection life.

That gives me a measure of hope. But our metaphors of the night and darkness are so strong that it remains hard to welcome darkness as a friend, to see benefits in night's depths. How can a soul's dark night be life-enhancing? Is it possible to look *forward* to the night and find *peace* in the darkness?

In her book *Learning to Walk in the Dark*, Barbara Brown Taylor suggests we can. She laments that many religious communities are overwhelmingly committed to a "full solar spirituality," all light and positivity. They want nothing to do with the dark. Protesting this half-baked approach, she sets forth another way, a "lunar spirituality," in which we learn lessons that only walking in the dark can teach us.

> ...new life starts in the dark. Whether it is a seed in the ground, a baby in the womb, or Jesus in the tomb, it starts in the dark.[8]

The Hours of prayer teach us to embrace darkness as part of each day's journey with God and as a source of life and well-being for us. Arising at night to pray, we discover a world profoundly different than we see in the daytime. Quiet. Cool. Damp. As John Ames observed, the night smells and feels different.

Perhaps we might even find comfort in the intimate embrace of a loving God there.

We have not known a god's vengeance. When his hand
closes over our wings, some kindliness makes a cave
of his palm, and we grow like mushrooms in great dark.[9]

BRIAN SWANN

Darkness may provide a refuge. A cave that shelters. A place of rest. A place where, as Brian Swann suggests, our roots can feed "on light laid down aeons ago." We can take solace in the night. We may find it a place of surprising connection, rootedness, sustenance, and growth.

A gentle alarm awakens me. I reach out and fumble for my phone, hitting "stop" a few times until it takes. I flop back and look at the ceiling. It's 3:00 a.m., and I am a retreatant at Gethsemani Abbey.

Sitting on the side of the bed, I hold my head until the fog lifts, don my glasses, and walk to the bathroom to splash cold water on my face. I grab my sandals, tuck my shirt in, pick my hoodie off the back of the chair, put it on, and struggle to get the zipper lined up. I go back toward the light and—zip!—it's done. I snatch the room key from the desk and head out the door.

My room is close to the church balcony, just out my door and then a few steps across a stone floor. I see about ten other sleepy night-pilgrims gathered. Picking up the printed liturgy, I sit, locate "Wednesday Vigils," breathe and wait. Most of the monks are in place. A few stragglers shuffle in in silence.

Bells ring. The organ sounds. "Lord, come to my assistance," one monk chants. The rest respond: "Lord, make haste to help me." Voices are a bit flat from nighttime throats. Mine is squeaky, and I keep the volume at a whisper. After a psalm inviting us to join those who serve God in the night watches, the monks sing a hymn. The melody is simple, pretty, and consoling.

A spoken service follows. Responsively, we read psalms that portray people in distress crying out to God, pleading for divine intervention. A brief reading from a saint's sermon, a prayer, the commemoration of our Lady Mary, the benediction, and we're done. For fifteen minutes in the wee hours, we have lifted our voices to God, affirming: "Yours is the day and yours is the night."

I return to my room. I'm awake now, so I read for a bit. Eventually, losing focus, I close my eyes and sleep for an hour or two. I am at rest, calm, reassured.

The silence of the barn at evening,
when the shepherd draws shut the door
and starts home for the night, is heavenly,
for it says almost aloud that every lamb
is found, every ewe has found her lamb
and is feeding, and is content.[10]

WENDELL BERRY

Those who pray Vigils, the night prayers, have learned to embrace darkness and find peace in the night. The psalms they chant are entirely realistic about dangers that threaten us but equally concerned to help us take our fears to God in prayerful lament, petition, and song.

My eyes are awake before each watch of the night,
that I may meditate on your promise.

PSALM 119:148

Praying against the deeper darkness

As I go back and read what I've written about darkness, I see my limited perspective. I write from a place of safety and privilege. My fears, real and imagined, don't begin to represent a full picture of nighttime dread. We must never downplay how frightening the darkness can actually be for people who must face much deeper darkness and who understand better than I "the terror of the night" (Psalm 91:5).

Tonight, people will huddle alone or with their families, waiting for the next bomb to fall, the next soldier to break down their door. Others will try to sleep in crime-ridden or gang-controlled neighborhoods, never feeling safe. Vulnerable migrants and refugees seeking better, safer lives will be exposed to exploitation and harm. Their fears will multiply dramatically when the sun goes down in the strange, lonely places where they nervously bed down. May I never forget.

However, nor can I underestimate the human spirit and its ability to cope with even the deepest fears. Most people find ways to deal with what darkness can bring—or at least talk their way into a form of comfort that makes sense to them. Perhaps, for a moment, they find ways to quiet the dread within.

In *Letters and Papers from Prison*, World War II prisoner and pastor Dietrich Bonhoeffer describes being intrigued by how his fellow captives coped in the face of Allied bombing raids.

> In my time here I've been trying to observe how far people believe in anything "supernatural." Three ideas seem to be widespread, each being partly expressed in some superstitious practice: (1) Time after time one hears "Keep your fingers crossed," some sort of power being associated with the accompanying thought: people do not want to feel alone in times of danger, but to be sure of some invisible presence. (2) "Touch wood" is the exclamation every evening, when the question is discussed "whether they will come tonight or not"; this seems to be a recollection of the wrath of God on the hubris of man, a metaphysical, and not merely a moral reason for humility. (3) "If it's got your number on, you'll get it," and therefore everyone may as well stay where he is.... To the last mentioned we might add another remark

> that is very often heard here: "Who knows what good may come of it?"[11]

Bonhoeffer tries to interpret his fellow prisoners' clichés from a theological perspective. He concludes that something in us all reaches out for larger meanings and invisible supports when terror befalls us.

In another passage, Bonhoeffer takes direct aim at the prison authorities and records how they might have helped those terrified prisoners but only made things worse for them during the night raids.

> There are no air-raid shelters for the prisoners. With all the labour available here, it would have been quite easy to provide these in good time. A dug-out has been built, but only for the authorities; apart from that, all that happens is that the prisoners on the top floor are locked in with the others in the ground-floor cells. When I asked why the prisoners in the second-floor cells were not moved down to the first floor, I was told that it would make too much work. There is no first-aid shelter. When the sick-bay was put out of action during a heavy attack, they could not start to bandage the injured till after it was over. No one who has experienced it will ever forget the shouting and screaming of the locked-up prisoners during a heavy air raid.... Seven hundred soldiers are exposed here to the dangers of a bombing attack with no protection.[12]

The Bible records human injustice like this and rails against it. The psalms recited during Vigils are not shy about it. They were given to people in times like Bonhoeffer and his fellow prisoners faced. The exile community, in enemy hands, had lost everything and likewise lived at the mercy of their captors.

Walter Brueggemann reminds us that the psalms still speak to the sufferings of those who are treated unjustly by the powerful.

> ...the faith to which the Psalms bear witness is concerned with the dynamics of power. Petitioners in the Psalms plead with God to redress societal and relational wrongs as the covenant God who brings justice, and so the portrayal of YHWH in these texts is of a God who is engaged with this community—a God in the fray.[13]

As we pray at night or lie in bed unable to sleep, focused on our own fears, worries, doubts, and apprehensions, let us also remember those facing darker, more life-threatening forms of injustice, terror, and dread. Also, let us pray that those who can help will help. Each night let us ask the God of justice and love "to give light to those who sit in darkness and in the shadow of death" (Luke 1:79).

Befriending the darkness

In the beginning, God separated darkness from light, but God did not remove the darkness completely. I believe this shows that God wants us to dance with creation at night as well as in the day.

After praying Vigils and before I went to my room to read, I made my way down to the dining hall for a glass of water. I could see the Abbey's peaceful grounds through the wall of windows. A single bulb lit the patio outside the building, but the path below was in shadows. I walked out to the wall by the birdfeeders and looked through the trees. A young man was walking the path in the quiet and dark.

It was so serene. I have never been anywhere as quiet at Gethsemani, and the night air amplified the silence. Watching the walker make his way around the path, I thought, "What a perfect place to walk, and what a perfect time." It was new moon—no light in the sky. Clouds covered the expanse, so no stars were in view.

Were it not for the patio light, the entire area would have been in complete darkness. I wished it had been. The meager human effort to illuminate the night contributed little to the scene. Once I was on the path, the glory belonged to the dark, the stillness, the peace. It felt friendly, welcoming, reassuring.

In his song, "Pacing the Cage," Bruce Cockburn says that we may unexpectedly find that darkness is our friend when our path leads us through the dark places. Perhaps we may embrace, even befriend, the night. The darkness, the stillness, the unseen life forms and forces all around us that keep our world going until daylight, the promise of a God who does not sleep and watches over it all; perhaps there is peace to be found here.

Maybe some kindliness has indeed made a cave in the dark hollow of Another's hand, where we may rest and find ourselves safe.

Remember...

Each day begins in the dark of night.
Darkness and light are both part of every day's journey.

Darkness is also a metaphor for the bad
and fearful things of life. It frightens us.

Even the strongest believers have gone through
periods of darkness in their faith and life.

We must always remember those who suffer
in the deep darkness of violence and injustice.

We may learn to befriend darkness as
a place where God holds us.

Consider...

What anxieties and fears have darkness
and nighttime elicited in you?

What are your nighttime habits?

Think about a "dark" time in your life.
What was that like? What brought you through?

In what ways do you think you might be
able to "befriend" darkness?

SOURCES

1. Taylor, Barbara Brown. *Learning to Walk in the Dark*. New York: HarperCollins Publishers, 2014.

2. Robinson, Marilynne.

3. Carrasco, Isabel. "Biphasic Sleep" (culturacolectiva.com/en/history/biphasic-sleep-medieval-two-sleep-shifts-history).

4. Henion, Leigh Ann. *Night Magic: Adventures Among Glowworms, Moon Gardens, and Other Marvels of the Dark*. Little, Brown and Company, Kindle Edition, 2024.

5. Henion, Leigh Ann.

6. Tolkien, J.R.R. *The Return Of The King: Being the Third Part of the Lord of the Rings*. HarperCollins, Kindle Edition, 2012.

7. Mother Teresa, undated letter (en.wikiquote.org/wiki/Mother_Teresa).

8. Taylor, Barbara Brown.

9. Swann, Brian. "Darkness and Deeper Dark," from *Poetry* (July 1969) (poetryfoundation.org/poetrymagazine/browse?volume=114&issue=4&page=31volume=114&issue=4&page=31).

10. Berry, Wendell. *A Small Porch: Sabbath Poems 2014 and 2015*. Catapult, Kindle Edition, 2016.

11. Bonhoeffer, Dietrich. *Letters and Papers from Prison*. Simon and Schuster: Touchstone updated edition, Kindle Edition, 2011.

12. Bonhoeffer, Dietrich.

13. Brueggemann, Walter; Bellinger, Jr., William H. *Psalms (New Cambridge Bible Commentary)*. Cambridge University Press, Kindle Edition, 2014.

Lauds

WELCOMING NEWNESS OF LIFE

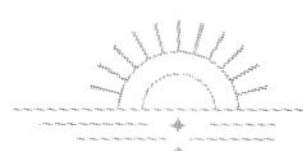

The steadfast love of the Lord never ceases,
his mercies never come to an end;
they are new every morning;
great is your faithfulness.

LAMENTATIONS 3:22–23

Awake, my soul! Awake, O harp and lyre!
I will awake the dawn.

PSALM 57:8

Let us awaken to the light: the world is full of God![1]

Pierre Teilhard de Chardin

Morning memories and the elusive routine

I have always had a conflicted relationship with mornings. As a "night person," I've found my best mindfulness and inspiration in dark solitude in the wee hours. It is hard to get excited about dawn when you fall asleep so close to daybreak.

Still, I have great morning memories. As a child I walked to elementary school. There were two ways I could go. The first followed streets up a hill to the school. The second took a shortcut through an old quarry, which required scaling a rock wall. I liked the adventurous route and can still sometimes visualize the grips and footholds I counted on for the climb. My parents never knew of my career as an alpinist.

When I was a young pastor in Vermont, I drove a small school bus. School was rarely cancelled in the winter, no matter how much snow had fallen. Rising before light, snowplows whizzing by, I went to my neighbor's where the bus was kept. He helped me put chains on the tires (I'm not very handy). Then off I'd go, winding around snow-covered gravel roads to pick up students. Such mornings helped me appreciate our community's spirit and neighbors who were always there to help a fledgling find his way.

When we visited Gail's grandparents in Ohio, mornings were lovely, peaceful, and life-affirming. We'd come to the table, spread by Grandma Anna with a delicious farmer's breakfast. We sat and Grandpa Jess would ask me to read from a devotional book. Then he would pray. I will always remember his grateful words: "Lord, thank you for sound minds and healthy bodies." Morning grace was tangible.

Unlike those dear saints whose morning habits were forged by life on the farm as well as by faith, I have struggled my whole life to have a consistent morning routine. In my faith tradition, "morning devotions" like I just described were commended as the best way to start the day. Habitually reading the Bible and praying in the morning were primary means of nurturing one's daily relationship with God. The earlier the better. Well, this faith "leader" failed to make it happen with any regularity.

I know people who don't need a morning alarm, and others who do but never hit snooze. These people wake up and they're awake. What's wrong with them? I struggle to rise, clear my head, and have anything resembling enthusiasm for life in the early hours. A kindred spirit wrote Proverbs 27:14: "Whoever blesses a neighbor with a loud voice, rising early in the morning, will be counted as cursing."

I have this nagging feeling, however, that I *should* start the day intentionally, with a health and faith-enhancing routine. It's engrained in our cultural DNA. We've heard it all our lives: "Early to bed, early to rise..." and something about being first in line at the worm buffet. You know what I mean.

An entire self-help industry, exemplified by Benjamin Spall and Michael Xander's chronicle of morning testimonies, *My Morning Routine: How Successful People Start Every Day Inspired*, affirms this.

> The way you spend your morning has an outsized effect on the rest of your day. The choices we make during the first hour or so of our morning determines whether we have productivity and peace of mind for the rest of the day, or whether it will clobber us over the head. Unfortunately for most of us, good days don't happen by accident. Unforeseen events will step forward to challenge your best-laid plans. If you don't dip into your inner reservoirs of energy, focus, and calm first thing, you won't

> stand a chance. Start your morning with intentionality, and you can then bring these "wins" with you into the rest of your day.[2]

The authors interviewed hundreds about their morning routines; as a rule, the people they talked to are privileged, high-capacity, entrepreneurial, driven folks with demanding careers and creative ambitions. They tackle life head-on, living at a fast pace with lots of responsibility. They have homes, businesses, partners, and families to care for. There are not many traditionally religious among them, though spirituality pervades their lives. They seem thoroughly integrated into the flow of upper-middle-class capitalist, therapeutic culture.

I am impressed with how attentive most of them are to carve out time each day for truly important things, like caring for their bodily and mental health, tending to close relationships, and fulfilling personal priorities. I admire their discipline to say "no" and their wisdom in knowing when to say it. Many train like athletes to keep themselves on track.

Although many of those interviewed are tech-y people, they are well aware of tech's dangers and its ability to distract from healthy participation in face-to-face life. They do not constantly look at their screens or check emails, social media, or news. Most are ruthless about putting their devices away to more fully engage in life, work, and relationships. Watching TV is rarely mentioned. They get enough sleep (averaging 7.5 hours). When they access news, it's often through print sources. They take time to slow down and tend to what's important. Because many have days that are fast-paced and filled with duties, they focus on morning (or whenever their day starts) as prime time for mindfulness.

Spall and Xander's subjects are realists about allowing for individual differences and changing circumstances, graciously advising self-charity when it comes to maintaining a morning routine. They warn against becoming "militaristic" about any method and show little angst over their own "failures." I love the woman who says, "Simply getting out of bed can be a victory." She uses prayer to remind herself "today is a gift, no matter how I use it." That makes me feel better.

However, I just entered a new season of life (retirement from my full-time job), and I know it's a perfect time to develop new morning habits. Without the pressure of daily work responsibilities, I have a chance to create a new normal for how I might approach each day more aware. We'll see how it goes.

> You fool, it is life that makes you dance: have you forgotten? Come out of the smoke, the world is tossing in its sleep, the sun is up, the land is bursting in the silence of dawn. The gentle earth relaxes and spreads out to embrace the strong sun. The grasses and flowers speak their own secret names.[3] ▪ THOMAS MERTON

Each day: a gift, an adventure

One thing I know from experience: each day waits with marvels to be explored. God's mercies are "new every morning." Wonder dances all through creation and in the midst of daily life. Morning brings a new beginning, providing fresh chances to discover life's marvels. As Macrina Widerkehr says, "Morning is a call to our own resurrection...."[4]

A favorite meditation by Eugene Peterson reinforces this:

> We wake up each morning to a world we did not make. How did it get here? How did we get here? We open our eyes and see that "old bowling ball the sun" careen over the horizon. We wiggle our toes. A mocking bird takes off and improvises on themes set down by robins, vireos,

> and wrens, and we marvel at the intricacies. The smell of frying bacon works its way into our nostrils and we begin anticipating buttered toast, scrambled eggs, and coffee freshly brewed from our favorite Javanese beans.
>
> There's so much here—around, above, below, inside, outside. Even with the help of poets and scientists we can account for very little of it. We notice this, then that. We start exploring the neighborhood. We try this street, and then that one. We venture across the tracks. Before long we are looking out through telescopes and down into microscopes, curious, fascinated by this endless proliferation of sheer Isness — color and shape and texture and sound.[5] ▪ **EUGENE PETERSON**

Each day is a gift. It's all a gift. Pure gift. We awaken, and life, already in motion, invites us to join in. Although we rightly pride ourselves in the work we do, what we achieve, and the lives we make through responsible living, if we stop to think about it, that's only a part of the story. A mysterious Source and a whole context of life surrounds and supports the small parts we play.

As Psalm 100 affirms, it is God who made us, and not we ourselves. The Torah reminds that when we are tempted to say, "My power and the might of my own hand have gotten me this wealth," we must "remember the Lord [our] God, for it is he who gives [us] power to get wealth" (Deuteronomy 8:17–18). It is in God, Paul says, that we "live and move and have our being" (Acts 17:28). Any work we do, any good we advance, any status we achieve, is all done in the context of the giftedness of life. We didn't originate or create any of it, we don't really control much of it, and we don't have ultimate say in how it all turns out. It comes to us as a gift to be received. A gift for which we say, "Thank you." A gift to steward. A gift that has the capacity to astonish us each day.

Each day is an adventure. On her website, Adventure Wednesdays,[6] Stacey Newman Weldon said she used to think of adventure as backpacking through Nepal or some such exotic experience. Eventually, her definition became at once more mundane and expansive: to her now, an adventure is an event or experience that expands, shifts, or alters one's perspective or perception of their inner self or the outer world. As a verb, to adventure means to put oneself in situations, to challenge an inner fear, to let go of trying to control the outcome and to wonder at what surprise may show up.

To view each day as an adventure is to try and discover something that can bring new insight, promote personal growth, spark wonder and gratitude, or open up unexpected chances to serve. The ordinary challenges of daily living may lead to such a discovery. Maybe it will come through some special assignment given to us. We may initiate the discovery process. We may just stumble on one.

The growth or change that results may seem imperceptible, and at times we'll fall back a few steps. The goal is not to quantify the outcome. The glory of an adventure is to live it. Whatever change comes to me will grow organically out of the experience and will, in some way, become apparent. I need not name it.

Mary Oliver gets this. In her poem "Where Does the Temple Begin, Where Does It End?" she writes:

There are things you can't reach. But
you can reach out to them, and all day long.
The wind, the bird flying away. The idea of God.
And it can keep you as busy as anything else, and happier.
...I look; morning to night I am never done with looking.
Looking I mean not just standing around, but standing around

as though with your arms open.
And thinking: maybe something will come...[7]

Every morning mercies new. The monks at Gethsemani engage the dawn by laying hold of God's mercies during Lauds, the Hour of morning prayer. On weekdays, the Eucharist follows, so they not only praise God for mercies new but are also fed by them in the sacrament. Lauds reminds us that early morning is the time to welcome newness and feast on God's goodness as we prepare to live into a new day.

Though I prefer the stillness of the night watches, some of the brightest visions of wonder that I've received have come at dawn, when, with camera in hand, I've looked across country fields here in the Midwest to capture morning light refracted through pastel skies or hovering ghostlike layers of fog.

Where I live is nestled below a small rise leading from one plateau of farm fields to another. The land opens to lower-lying vistas to the east, which makes it a fine place to take pictures at sunrise. I love to go out when the midsummer fields are full of maturing crops. The sun breaks through the mist, reflecting off soybean leaves or corn stalks glistening with dew. I take something waterproof on which to kneel so I can get down low, close to the life stretching toward the orange glow. A steamy day might be in store, but at this hour a damp coolness prevails. I'm invigorated. I marvel at the light.

And the sounds! Early morning brings a resurrection of music, when birds awaken and their songs fill the air from the towering trees in our neighborhood. Before sunrise, it's too dark for birds to start foraging. However, they see well enough to perceive life and competitors nearby. So, they begin what scientists call "the dawn chorus." The singing birds communicate with other birds or their own chicks, signaling social position, defending territory, attracting mates, or reinforcing pair bonds. The dawn chorus begins as early as

4:00 a.m. and lasts until the choir completes its dawn cantata about thirty minutes after sunrise.

Where I live, robins, blackbirds, thrushes, finches, tits, wrens, sparrows, and doves lead the song. I am a novice listener, still learning to recognize which bird sings each part, but it is hard not to be impressed by this mass choir, unabashed in its exuberance, unapologetic about sounding reveille.

Morning has broken like the first morning,
blackbird has spoken like the first bird.
Praise for the singing!
Praise for the morning!
Praise for them, springing
fresh from the Word!
ELEANOR FARJEON

Sunday morning wonder at church

In the dawn years of my life, one place I found morning wonder was in Sunday worship at the Methodist church our family attended.

Rather than go to some block-walled classroom designed to relieve the congregation of fidgety kids, I wanted to stay with my parents in "big church" to see light streaming through stained glass, colorfully robed people processing, and the somber white-haired minister kneeling to pray. We joined the congregation's morning chorus, singing,

Glory be to the Father,
and to the Son and to the Holy Ghost.
As it was in the beginning, is now and ever shall be,
world without end. Amen.

My mom helped me follow the lyrics in the hymnal by tracing them with her finger. I wanted to be an acolyte carrying the flame, lighting the candles. I was as restless as any other kid, but what comes back to me is the wonder. Soon I was singing my first solo as a colorfully robed choir member in the balcony.

Sunday mornings in church birthed an entire imaginative world in my young soul. C.S. Lewis talked about "Joy"—the power of beauty and fairy tales to enchant and open up new worlds for us. Lewis was somewhat reclusive as a child, reading books and conjuring an imaginary world of "dressed animals" and "knights in armor." He wrote and illustrated his own stories. He felt the first stirrings of "Joy," a magical sense of things wondrous and real beyond this world's sensory experiences, in these moments.

> It would be far truer to say that fairy land arouses a longing for he knows not what. It stirs and troubles him (to his life-long enrichment) with the dim sense of something beyond his reach and, far from dulling or emptying the actual world, gives it a new dimension of depth. He does not despise real woods because he has read of enchanted woods: the reading makes all real woods a little enchanted.[8]

On Sunday mornings in church, I likewise found enchantment encountering worlds beyond through the bright colors and fresh breezes of grace felt in the worshipping community. Many of those moments seemed more "real" to me than this mundane world.

As I grew older, however, I became *dis*-enchanted. In the normal course of growing up, moving from innocence to experience, I put away childish things. Other activities and interests took the place of church, and my growing mind began questioning, then shaking off the naive faith of my younger years.

On the verge of adulthood, I was drawn to a new kind of faith, one more literalistic and zealous. I had a spiritual awakening near the end of high school and, behold, a new fundamentalist was born. This prosaic brand of faith touched me in a different way, but I realize now there was little place for imagination and wonder. In the born-again mindset, I forgot the Joy. I was falsely taught to look back on childhood as a time when I was ignorant and lost without God. I'm grateful for that awakening and the necessary turnaround in my life it brought at the time, but it took me decades to deconstruct the harmful box of fundamentalism into which my spirit had become contorted. It took me years to figure out that God had always been with me, even before I could understand or make conscious faith choices.

The narrow way of puritanical piety would never be enough, could never be enough. It didn't reveal a big enough God. It didn't help me imagine a big enough life. It did not lead me to envision a big enough vocation. It didn't enchant the world like my childhood experiences did. There was too little beauty, too little imagination, a noticeable lack of wonder.

Restless, I heard whispers about an "ancient-future" faith, with a renewed emphasis on liturgy, beauty, and a sacramental perspective in which the world is alive with God's glory. I read Robert Webber, who had left the fundamentalist church world to become an Episcopalian. He urged all Christians to rediscover rich, established ways of reenacting the gospel in worship even while pursuing new winds of the Spirit. I asked Dr. Webber to teach a workshop at our church. I was attracted to this ancient-future path.

The journey eventually led me to practice my faith in the Lutheran tradition. Along the way, I had my epiphany about how God had used Sunday morning wonder to speak to me from the beginning of my life. I realized that what I yearned for was nothing more ancient than the childhood where God first became known to me through the enchantment of Joy. As Parker Palmer writes,

> When we lose track of true self, how can we pick up the trail? One way is to seek clues in stories from our younger years, years when we lived closer to our birthright gifts.[9]

My "birthright gifts" came to me when I felt awe through stained glass and eternal flame. When my imagination was sparked by brilliant robes and the smell of old wood. When I was enchanted by the sturdy poetry of liturgy, the joy of song, and the embrace of community.

So, I embraced a more wonder-filled faith. I discarded prosaic methods of seeking God—decisional theology, biblicism, analytical theology, and methodistic piety. I concluded that faith involves taking my place in a Story best told through metaphor, venerable traditions, nature, and imagination-provoking art, music, and literature (including the Bible as sacred story, not instruction manual). I determined to see life, church, and the world as an arena in which to find *wonder* rather than answers.

In his book about "sacred sense," William P. Brown cites a practice Fred Craddock talked about.

> ...his ancestors would go out walking on Sunday afternoons, sometimes in groups, sometimes alone. They called it "going marveling." On these walks they would admire nature and collect unusual things—from rocks to wild flowers — to bring back home and share to the amazement of others.[10]

"Going marveling," as those good folks did, did not guarantee they would find wonder, but it put them in settings where it became more likely. The practice helped them pay attention, with hearts open to God's wonders in this very world. That's what I wanted: not the austere, life-denying faith that talked mostly about abandoning this world for another one.

Wonder. Imagination. Beauty. That's why I participate in worship on Sunday mornings now. Not to "have fellowship" with other believers. Not to "learn and grow" through studying the Bible. Not, heaven forbid, to fulfill some obligation. But to go marveling. To be where serendipity might happen. Marvels may come in a shaft of light through stained glass, the tears of a widow who's missing her husband, a child's smile, sweet wine at the Table, a hymn phrase so exquisite it makes me sigh, a few moments catching up with a friend's life, or a biblical narrative that draws me into the Story and worlds beyond.

> Sometimes I have loved the peacefulness of an ordinary Sunday. It is like standing in a newly planted garden after a warm rain. You can feel the silent and invisible life. All it needs from you is that you take care not to trample on it.[11] ■ MARILYNNE ROBINSON

Morning: creation and new creation

All year, every day, morning brings newness. Creation is reenacted. Additionally, Christians hold that a new creation was inaugurated through Jesus' life, death, and resurrection. That story is told in the seasons of the Church's Liturgical Year. Each day also represents the blessings associated with Jesus' story.

Every new day is a little Advent. The day lightens slowly, prophesied then proclaimed by the dawn chorus calling us to awaken. The bird sentinels sense the light's return. They herald hope.

Every new day is a little Christmas. A new birth takes place. The skies explode with light and song. A never-before experienced opportunity to know God's favor and peace is announced. The good news is for everyone and for all creatures and living things. God's love incarnate comes into a world awakening.

Every new day is a little Epiphany. I splash my body with cleansing waters of baptismal grace and rise to walk in new life. How will the light of truth and healing shine on me today? What opportunities to help repair the world will I encounter today? From whom might I receive or give grace and kindness today?

Every new day is a little Lent. Morning mist baptizes the earth with cool, invigorating hope. Sap flows through trunks and branches. Flowers begin pushing through the soil. I plough the hard earth of my heart, loosen and aerate it, prepare it for sowing, the warming sun, refreshing rains.

Every new day is a little Good Friday. Life awakens where death has created and nourished fertile soil. "All creatures die into it, and they live by it," says Wendell Berry. The morning that renews my life also gives me opportunity to die this same day—to love sacrificially so others might live.

Every new day is a little Easter. Life surprises! We walk into each sunrise not knowing what messenger might have good news for us, what unrecognized gardener might speak our name, what stranger we might meet on the road who will make our hearts burn within us, what unimaginable force might pass through locked doors to assuage our doubts, what witness we might share to give hope to others.

Every new day is a little Pentecost. Each day brings new creation. The Spirit moves over the darkness, and there is light! All creatures speak in tongues of praise. We live, move, and have our being in a reality greater than ourselves. We breathe, open our eyes, and the dance of new life begins.

The morning hours introduce us to the wonders of both creation and new creation. I relish the wonder. However, I'm still working on the waking up.

My spirit is willing. I'm told if you want to become a morning person, have a baby or get a dog. No more babies, but I am watching my son's dog this week, and it's (kind of) working.

> Here is an unspeakable secret: paradise is all around us and we do not understand. It is wide open. The sword is taken away, but we do not know it: we are off "one to his farm and another to his merchandise." Lights on. Clocks ticking. Thermostats working. Stoves cooking. Electric shavers filling radios with static. "Wisdom," cries the dawn deacon, but we do not attend.[12]
>
> ■ **THOMAS MERTON**

Remember...

God's mercies come to us new every morning.

There are benefits of having a healthy, disciplined morning routine. Some of us struggle to do that.

Each day is a pure gift and an adventure waiting to be experienced.

Sunday mornings in church worship may provide some of us with opportunities to experience wonder.

Just as God created the world in the beginning, and inaugurated a new creation in Christ, each day both are reenacted, promising newness, abundance, and blessing.

Consider...

What is your morning routine like? Would you call yourself a morning or night person? How do you prepare yourself each morning to face the day?

What are some of the good experiences you have had in early mornings?

Have you attended Sunday morning church services? What have your experiences been like?

How does your own faith journey influence the way you now approach living each day?

SOURCES

1. Deignan, Kathleen, CND; Osgood, Libby, CND.

2. Spall, Benjamin; Xander, Michael. *My Morning Routine: How Successful People Start Every Day Inspired*. Penguin Publishing Group, Kindle Edition, 2018.

3. Merton Thomas. "Atlas and the Fatman," in *The Behavior of Titans*. New Directions, First Edition, 1961.

4. Wiederkehr, Macrina. *Seven Sacred Pauses: Living Mindfully through the Hours of the Day*. Ave Maria Press, Kindle Edition, 2008.

5. Peterson Eugene H., *Christ Plays in Ten Thousand Places: A Conversation in Spiritual Theology*. Wm. B. Eerdmans Publishing Co, 2005.

6. Weldon, Stacey Newman (adventurewednesdays.com/lifes-an-adventure-adventure-is-life-the-definition-of-adventure).

7. Mary Oliver. "Why I Wake Early," in *Why I Wake Early: New Poems*. Beacon Press, Kindle Edition, 2004.

8. Lewis, C.S. "Dipping into Myth" (www.cslewis.com/dipping-into-myth).

9. Palmer, Parker J. *Let Your Life Speak: Listening for the Voice of Vocation*. Wiley, Kindle Edition, 2024.

10. Brown, William P. *Sacred Sense: Discovering the Wonder of God's Word and World*. Wm. B. Eerdmans Publishing Company, 2015.

11. Robinson, Marilynne.

12. Merton, Thomas. *Conjectures of a Guilty Bystander* (Image Classic). Random House Publishing Group, Kindle Edition, 1965/1966.

The Little Hours of Terce, Sext, None

VOCATION AND OUR DAILY WORK

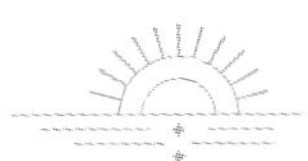

Little Hour One: *Terce*

For you, O Lord, have made me glad by your work;
at the works of your hands I sing for joy.

PSALM 92:4

People go out to their work and
to their labor until the evening.

PSALM 104:23

Knowing what you know
about yourself and the world,
what are you going to do?[1]

STEVEN GARBER

The "Little Hours" – The workday

Terce, the time for morning prayer in the Divine Hours, indicates the "third" hour of the day: 9:00 a.m. In our culture, that is the stereotypical designation for the beginning of the workday, which we describe as "nine to five."

The next two Hours, Sext and None, come at noon and 3:00 p.m. Together, Terce, Sext, and None cover the typical time for our daily work. Yes, people work a variety of shifts and at different times, but 9 to 5 is still common. The Divine Hours of prayer were set to fit this pattern.

Terce, Sext, and None are called "The Little Hours" because they are not universally observed, as morning and evening prayers are. These "Little Hours" together help us consider aspects of our human vocation (or calling) and the specific vocations that are played out in our daily work.

The Creation Liturgy portrays God at work. It also gives a foundational understanding of human work. Exposure to the monks at Gethsemani has given me additional insights about daily labor. My Gethsemani coffee mug is inscribed with the words *Ora et Labora* (pray and work), a Benedictine motto. "Spiritual" activities and manual labors alike have dignity and worth.

In the *National Catholic Register*, Father Dwight Longenecker unpacks the motto Ora et Labora. Because the physical world is real and matters, he says, labor keeps us connected to reality. Hard work "takes us out of our heads," helping us face temptations a contemplative life can bring: "fanciful head games, purely intellectual debates, mystical fantasies or spiritual sentimentality." It is meaningful because we work with God to bring forth good things from the earth. There is also a penitential aspect—the sweat, toil, and unfinished nature of work remind us that life and sanctity are not easy but require intense effort and dependence on God and others.

Father Longenecker also testifies that he discovers rich spiritual symbolism when he works:

> When I pull weeds in the garden, I confess my failings and pull the weeds from the garden of my soul. When I wash dishes I ask God to wash me thoroughly for I am a vessel of the Holy Spirit. When I gather the sheep in from the fields I pray that the Good Shepherd may gather me home at last.[2]

Adding to what the good priest says, let's remember that our *labora* extends to responsibilities that are broader than what we do for employment. As Steven Garber reminds us:

> Most of us cannot and do not live extraordinary lives. Instead we live in families and in neighborhoods, working and worshiping week by week in rhythms that make the sum of our lives, season after season, year after year. Life cannot be other than that.[3]

We have many vocations or "callings" that relate to the "stations" we hold in life. Garber points to our families, neighborhoods, worship communities, and other relationships that set the "rhythms" of our life. He also draws attention to the various seasons and years of our lives. Our work changes as life changes. But it is always true, as Vaclav Havel regularly said, that "the secret of man is the secret of his responsibility." To be a human being alive is to consider what my human vocation and specific vocational responsibilities require of me in my own stations and seasons of life.

From law to chocolate (and more)

Shawn Askinosie never worked 9 to 5 in his life. His energy and capacity defied limits. Here's how he described his life and work before he had a vocational turnaround:

> ...when I was sixteen, I began working after school every day for a local lawyer, and I became Missouri Boys State governor. After that I qualified for the National Speech and Debate Tournament. While still in high school, I became a congressional page in the U.S. House of Representatives. After my freshman year in college, I volunteered for the American embassy in Thailand during the Vietnam refugee crisis. I subsequently spent a year of college in Japan. I maintained this pace into adulthood, keeping incredibly, sometimes manically, busy, usually with things that truly engaged me and that I felt good about doing.
>
> Eventually, I became a successful criminal defense lawyer just like my dad. I spent the next two decades making money, winning seemingly impossible jury trials that were broadcast on Court TV, gaining prominence and recognition from national media outlets, and generally achieving things....[4]

Then, at a key moment in his life, Askinosie had the beginnings of an awakening. In the midst of his full-bore, Type A life, Shawn went on retreat at a Trappist monastery in Missouri to see the room where his father had spent the last night of his life before coming home and dying in Shawn's presence. Shawn had been a young teenager then. Now, years later, on this retreat he began a conversation with his father's death and the sorrow he had never processed. Little did he know it would lead him in a whole new direction in his life and work.

Shawn Askinosie's exploration of his grief gave him an appreciation of the wisdom of Kahlil Gibran:

> Kahlil Gibran wrote, "Our greatest joy is sorrow unmasked." It took me twenty-five years to figure that out. Gibran understood that joy can be found, and if not found then cultivated, via a deep acknowledgment of our sorrows. He knew that the exploration of heartbreak—our own, and the world's—leads to an expansive understanding of our true self. He knew that there, we can create meaning.[5]

As he worked through his grief, Shawn found his legal work more challenging. One particularly wrenching case, along with some unsettling health distress signals, led to a breaking point. The high-powered attorney realized he no longer loved his work. It no longer fit the person he was becoming.

Shawn began visiting the palliative care unit at a local hospital. There he discovered new things about himself through simply being with others and listening to their stories. He started pondering the idea of "vocation." Where did his gifts, his passions, and the world's need come together? What should he do? For five years, he prayed every day, "Dear God, please give me something else to do." He searched and researched, hoping for an epiphany that would tell him, "This is it!" But it never came. Along the way, he found guidance in the words of Thomas Merton:

> Discovering vocation does not mean scrambling toward some prize just beyond my reach but accepting the treasure of true self I already possess. Vocation does not come from a voice "out there" calling me to be something I am not. It comes from a voice "in here" calling me to be the person I was born to be, to fulfill the original selfhood given me at birth by God.[6]

One day, as Askinosie was driving to a funeral near his grandparents' old farm, he thought about his family heritage of producing and providing food for others and his recent new interest in baking and making chocolate desserts. An idea emerged: "What about making chocolate from scratch?" He had no idea what that involved, but the thought eventually flowered into a business called Askinosie Chocolate.

> I started a small-batch chocolate factory at the forefront of the American craft chocolate boom....By establishing close, just, trusting relationships with everyone with whom we do business, my team and I find a deep sense of purpose, and terrific pleasure, in our work....
>
> My exploration of my deepest sorrow allowed me to uncover passions I didn't know I had. Ultimately, it led me to the discovery of my vocation, and to the creation of Askinosie Chocolate.[7]

If you are anything like me, you didn't see that coming! Making chocolate? However, a closer look shows that, for Shawn Askinosie, it has never been just about making chocolate. Shawn developed a conviction that the world needs talented, thoughtful craftspeople devoted to practices of building relationships, helping others find dignity in their work, and serving those in need, He found a way to live out his truest self, to fulfill his vocation and create a company with a collective sense of vocation as well. The company mission statement summarizes this vocation.

> We at Askinosie Chocolate exist to craft exceptional chocolate while serving our farmers, our customers, our neighborhood, and one another, striving in all we do to leave whatever part of the world we touch better for the encounter.[8]

Vocation: the masks of God and the wondrous web

The Little Hour of Terce calls us to begin our daily work with mindfulness. How do we approach who we are and what we do each day? Employed people spend vast amounts of time engaged in job-related activities. In addition, we have daily duties that don't come with a paycheck. No one can afford to be inattentive to the meaning of vocation and work. It's an essential part of being human.

"Vocation" means a "calling," and in Christian theology it refers to a primary way God works through human beings in the world. God creates us with talents, abilities, and personalities, and God forms us through our experiences. Then God calls us to use these gifts to serve our neighbors and the world around us. As we do, God works in and through us to promote life and human flourishing.

People have multiple vocations. Our callings grow out of our "stations in life"—for example, we have relationships and roles within our families. At school, we are called to be students. Our job is another calling. We are citizens in our local communities and within society and the world at large. We belong to faith communities and other organizations in which we are called to serve.

Gene Veith notes that the reformer Martin Luther taught passionately about Christian vocation:

> ...in his earthly kingdom, just as in his spiritual kingdom, God bestows his gifts through means. God ordained that human beings be bound together in love, in relationships and communities existing in a state of interdependence. In this context, God is providentially at work caring for his people, each of whom contributes according to his or her God-given talents, gifts, opportunities, and stations. Each thereby becomes what Luther terms a "mask of God": "All our work in the field, in the garden, in the city, in the home, in struggle, in government – to what does it all amount before God except child's play, by means of which God is pleased to give his gifts in the field, at home, and everywhere? These are the masks of our Lord God, behind which he wants to be hidden and to do all things."[9]

A thought experiment

I hold in my hand a bus ticket. Waiting at the station, I am greeted by a woman behind the counter, who directs me to the right location. A man with a broom and dustpan tidies up around the room, which is filled with early morning travelers. It is just past 3:00 a.m., and we look it. Buses are lined up outside, ready for us to board. When it's time, the bus driver opens the door, makes his announcement, and checks our tickets. Passengers and luggage safely aboard, he greets us over the sound system, outlines the course of our trip, backs out, and we are off.

I think about what it takes for one passenger like me to make a trip like this.

People designed and oversee the website for purchasing tickets. Financial services workers process my order securely. This depends on a reliable electrical grid, computers and servers, and wires and switches that send and receive the signals. Someone made those things, transported them, installed them. Someone maintains them. People designed my computer and the smartphone that displays my ticket. Workers manufactured them, others marketed them, still others worked in the store that stocked and sold them. That same electrical grid lights the station where I wait for the bus. Water and sewer systems keep it hygienic. Maintenance workers keep it clean and functioning.

And now we're on the road. People designed and built this bus. Workers manufactured and assembled thousands of parts to form it. It runs on refined fuel that human beings harvested, processed, blended, and carried to filling stations in other vehicles made by human hands. The road we take did not just appear in the wilderness. People built it from materials produced within another ecosystem of workers. Citizens pay taxes into a complex governmental and contractual system full of workers that keep the road maintained.

I could go on and on, but after considering just a few particulars, I find this exercise virtually endless. If I go far enough, I might ultimately get back to the beginning and hear God say, "It is good."

People talk about heading out of civilization to "God's country," where nature displays awe-inspiring vistas. I like to do that too. But here I am today, riding this bus, inspired by Luther's God hidden behind a maze of human masks. The complexity and interconnectivity exceed the scope of my imagination. How marvelous are God's works! They are past finding out!

Life depends on a wondrous web of people fulfilling their vocations, from sweeper to driver, bus manufacturer to builder of roads, IT person to store clerk. Each masks the grace of God, who keeps this world functioning through them. God works through our hands. You and I are parts of a "wondrous web" of vocation. Through our daily work, no matter how insignificant it may seem, God cares for the world. There is dignity in it all.

But let's step back for a moment and see how our daily work fits into an even greater plan.

The human calling: baptism and vocation, furthering *shalom*

Defining vocation primarily in terms of daily work may obscure something greater. Beyond the stations of life I'm in and the work I do, I have a larger calling as a human being created by God.

Before I ask, "What should I do?" I have to ask, "Who am I?" My identity is more fundamental than the work I do. In Christian tradition, baptism answers this question. At Jesus' baptism, Matthew 3:16–17 says:

> And when Jesus had been baptized, just as he came up from the water, suddenly the heavens were opened to him and he saw the Spirit of God descending like a dove and alighting on him. And a voice from heaven said, "This is my Son, the Beloved, with whom I am well pleased."

In baptism, God named Jesus as his beloved Son. God likewise claims us, through baptism, as beloved children. We are cleansed, renewed, and affirmed as God's daughters and sons. The ritual of baptism gives public witness to what is true of all people created, loved, and redeemed by God.

Furthermore, in the act of baptism, God made a public pronouncement about Jesus' unique calling. When God declared Jesus the "Son," this referred not only to Jesus' relationship with God. "Son" is a kingly title (Psalm 2:7), indicating Jesus' enthronement as God's promised Messiah. To confirm this, the Spirit descended and anointed Jesus as he rose from the waters.

It was only after this strong affirmation of identity and vocation that Jesus went out and began his daily work of teaching, healing, and fighting the powers that threaten human well-being.

In the same way, baptism and vocation answer these basic questions in life for you and me. My identity? I am God's beloved child. I belong to God and am loved. God takes pleasure in me. My vocation? I bear a calling as a unique human being in the world. I am to live out this calling, representing God in every station of my life and in every vocational responsibility.

Let me put these distinctions in a list to help us see the whole picture:

- *My identity:* God's beloved child, uniquely made and gifted.
- *My vocation:* My human calling to represent God and live out my identity in every aspect of life.
- *My stations in life:* The various arenas of life in which I live and work.
- *My vocations:* The callings and responsibilities I have to fulfill in my stations of life.
- *My daily work:* The work I do each day in an effort to fulfill all of the above.

The human vocation

Genesis 1 calls humans "the image of God" in the world. Ancient Near East temples displayed a statue of the god each temple represented. When devotees came to the temple, they knew their religious duties because they saw the image and remembered what that particular god required of them. The Creation Liturgy teaches that human beings are the image of the God who created heaven and earth as his temple. The human vocation is to represent the Creator and to call all creatures to live in God's blessing.

The Creation Liturgy also outlines our specific assignment:

> God blessed them, and God said to them, "Be fruitful and multiply, and fill the earth and subdue it; and have dominion over the fish of the sea and over the birds of the air and over every living thing that moves upon the earth." ■ GENESIS 1:28

Humans are God's stewards in this world: their role is to protect and care for it so that God's blessing might fill the earth. We live in a world of both possibility and peril. Humans, who by God's blessing multiply and fill the earth, are to "subdue" chaotic elements that threaten creation's well-being. We are to "have dominion" over the world and its resources, but not by lording over the world to exploit it. Rather, we give attention to it, nurture and guard it so all life may flourish. This goal is described by the Hebrew word *shalom*. What God wants most for creation is shalom.

Shalom is usually translated as "peace," but it points to something more profound than that. Shalom indicates wholeness and integrity in all of our relationships. Shalom points to human flourishing. We are enough. We have enough, we are loved, we are safe. Shalom signifies that all is well and right.

Cornelius Plantinga of Calvin College put it this way:

> [The biblical prophets] dreamed of a new age in which crookedness would be straightened out, rough places made plain. The foolish would be made wise, and the wise, humble. They dreamed of a time when the deserts would flower, the mountains would stream with red wine, a time when weeping would be heard no more, and when people could sleep without weapons on their laps. People could work in peace, their work having meaning and point. A wolf could lie down with

> a lamb....All nature would be fruitful, benign, and filled with wonder upon wonder; all humans would be knit together in brotherhood and sisterhood; and all nature and all humans would look to God, walk with God, lean toward God, and delight in God....
>
> The webbing together of God, humans, and all creation in justice, fulfillment, and delight is what the Old Testament prophets called shalom.[10]

Shalom has been God's intention for creation from the beginning. Human beings were put here to advance and sustain a state of shalom. Jesus affirmed this when he said, "Blessed are the peacemakers, for they will be called children of God." Our blessed privilege is to be shalom-promoters.

The prophet Micah summarized how we go about this human Vocation:

> *He has told you, O mortal, what is good;*
> *and what does the Lord require of you*
> *but to do justice, and to love kindness,*
> *and to walk humbly with your God?*
>
> **MICAH 6:8**

Also, Jesus pointed to the "greatest commandment" as the path to fulfilling our calling.

> [Jesus] said to him, "You shall love the Lord your God with all your heart, and with all your soul, and with all your mind." This is the greatest and first commandment. And a second is like it: "You shall love your neighbor as yourself." On these two commandments hang all the law and the prophets. ■ **MATTHEW 22:37–40**

No matter what other callings, jobs, or occupations I may have in life, texts like this help me understand my primary vocation as a human being living daily in this world. I am to be a person who pursues shalom for myself, others, and the world around me through practicing justice, kindness, and a humble faith. By loving God and acting in love toward my neighbor.

What specific work am I to do?

Work, actual work, is central to most people's lives. Assuming forty years of full-time employment, we spend about 80,000 hours in work activity over a lifetime. However, many struggle with figuring out specifically what to do for a job. At this time in history, when we have much more freedom to choose what to do, trying to find one's path can provoke angst. Work not only provides income, it's also an essential part of our self-image, helping us understand how we fit in the world and connect to others.

Having said that, I know that people approach work and its importance in their life differently.

My wife and I have a strong sense of vocation due to our faith backgrounds, which emphasized God's calling and serving others through our work. I recognize that other folks are not so obsessed with work or career. They work to live; they don't live to work. Their jobs provide for them and their family. They do something for which they have ability and a measure of interest, but it's not the most important thing in their lives. They do their best, but they don't invest high levels of emotional energy in their job. That passion is reserved for avocations outside of work. Their paid career is there mostly to support what's truly important to them. And that's okay.

Some who teach vocation don't always seem to affirm that this is okay. A well-known adage states that a person's calling is found at the intersection of their strongest passions and the world's deepest needs. A statement like that can be intimidating. It can promote an idealistic "missionalism" that views all work in grand categories. The missionalists among us, along with the Type As, workaholics, and careerists, sometimes seem intent on having us all change into superhero outfits and courageously change the world. Some of us may just want to change spark plugs and then go home to our real lives.

Parker Palmer calls this "vocationalism." He reflects on his own experience of it in his religious tradition:

> ...the idea of "vocation" I picked up in those circles created distortion until I grew strong enough to discard it. I mean the idea that vocation, or calling, comes from a voice external to ourselves, a voice of moral demand that asks us to become someone we are not yet—someone different, someone better, someone just beyond our reach....
>
> Today I understand vocation quite differently—not as a goal to be achieved but as a gift to be received. Discovering vocation does not mean scrambling toward some prize just beyond my reach but accepting the treasure of true self I already possess. Vocation does not come from a voice "out there" calling me to become something I am not. It comes from a voice "in here" calling me to be the person I was born to be, to fulfill the original selfhood given me at birth by God.[11]

We are all called to fulfill the human vocation as God's image in the world. But how I do that specifically comes down to who I am as an individual and what talents, interests, and opportunities I have. I am called to be myself and make best use of the gifts I've been given. That is not self-centeredness. It is responsible gratitude for the lives we've actually been given. Palmer refers to an old Hasidic tale:

> Rabbi Zusya, when he was an old man, said, "In the coming world, they will not ask me: 'Why were you not Moses?' They will ask me: 'Why were you not Zusya?'"[12]

Many struggle to find work that fits their identity. Some folks figure out early on who they are, their interests, and where their talents can be used effectively. They may end up with long careers in business, industry, or service. Others never find their niche, bouncing around, trying different things without success. Still others spend a life doing work that may not be deeply meaningful to them but which enables them to pursue interests they deem more important than a job. Finding one's "fit" can involve a journey.

My vocational journey...

I recently retired from my full-time occupation as a hospice chaplain. This gives me a timely opportunity for reflection. I believe God called me to work as a hospice chaplain, but doing so required a journey.

In youth, I received little vocational counsel. I was a white suburban privileged American baby boomer: my father commuted to the office and provided for us while mom stayed home and ran the household. My teachers were my vocational models, as I saw them working every day. Having an innate love for learning, especially in the liberal arts, I developed a vague notion of becoming a teacher. Odd jobs I worked to have spending money did not lead to any such musings. My main interest was sports. I was a decent athlete and my love was baseball. Despite some success in high school, no one ever helped me identify a path to being a professional ballplayer or working in sports.

I had a spiritual awakening as a high school senior after a disorienting relocation. It signified a profound turnaround in my life, and I became obsessed with studying the Bible. When Jesus called fishermen to follow him, they abandoned their boats, splashed to shore, and never looked back. Likewise, I set out on a new path. After auditing some Bible college courses, I decided I would study for ministry.

My dad had a talk with me, suggesting I go to a different college first and become qualified for another profession. He was rightly concerned that my youthful zeal might wane and I would have nothing to fall back on. But I wouldn't hear of it. I had decided to follow Jesus, and there was no turning back.

The strict fundamentalist Bible college I attended provided necessary structure for this immature and inexperienced kid. I soon made a minor adjustment in my vocational plans when I decided to pursue being a senior pastor rather than a youth minister, like I had first envisioned. Studying and teaching the Bible to the whole church was the overriding preoccupation of my institution, and I caught the fever.

Before I knew it, I was a twenty-two-year-old novice pastor in a two-hundred-year-old Baptist church in the Vermont hills. It was a small village, and an even smaller congregation, but it was a big new world to me. A single pew in that old church knew more about being a minister than I did. I fumbled around and learned what no school or the Bible itself could teach me. I learned about living in a community of people. They taught me lifelong lessons, putting up with my immaturity, ignorance, and inexperience.

I was asked to officiate a lot of funeral services for folks in that village. I did services for infants and elderly, for non-church-attenders to the congregation's most faithful members, from Vermonters rooted there for generations to "flatlanders" with vacation homes in the hills. I'm not sure how comforting or insightful these services were, but from the beginning of my adult life and work, I became acquainted with grief and provided rituals that sought to help people through it. A seed was planted.

We eventually moved back to Chicago so I could pursue a seminary degree. I considered reexploring teaching, but my professors encouraged me to see that serving in a church would be more satisfying and influential than being cloistered in an academic setting. It was reaffirmed—I would be Pastor Mike.

While I was in seminary, our church's minister resigned. The congregation asked me to serve, and I did so for several years while other duties were calling me too. Children were filling our home. I worked factory jobs when funding for school dried up. Life was becoming more complicated.

I decided to take a course for seminary in Clinical Pastoral Education (CPE) at a local hospital. The medical world had always intrigued me, and I found pastoral visiting in healthcare settings meaningful. CPE, designed for training chaplains, added new clinical and community-service dimensions to my understanding of "pastor."

I responded like Shawn Askinosie did when he took up hospital work among the chronically ill and dying. He would simply visit and sit with people, listen to their stories, and take interest in the details of their lives. He found that most welcomed a prayer, and when he asked their prayer concerns, they would share some of their deepest concerns and dreams. After praying for them, Shawn would feel a deep joy and the sense that he was right where he was supposed to be.

CPE was a high point in my seminary years, but I wasn't attentive enough to hear any kind of career guidance in the experience. I finished the course, went on to complete seminary with honors and the preaching award, and had a mindset still focused on being a pastor with an emphasis on teaching.

We moved to Indianapolis, where I served on staff in a suburban evangelical church. For ten years, we raised our family and participated in the life of the congregation. Gail, also on a vocational journey, returned to school for a degree in counseling. I focused on teaching, leading worship and music in the church, and participating in mission trips around the world while our family was growing up.

Oh, and one other thing returned: baseball. Our boys started playing Little League and I became a coach. I had long taught that

Christians' lives should not revolve around the "temple" (the church organization) but should be engaged in the life of the broader community. I took up the challenge of doing just that, through coaching my boys in the game I love so much. My relationships with friends at the ball fields became as important as, or more important than, what I was doing in the church's program.

I also continued to visit people in the hospital, officiate funerals, and develop my understanding of pastoral care in ministry. This eventually contributed to the biggest vocational change in my life. Dear friends in the school and baseball community had a son who developed a brain tumor. Daniel went through a year-and-a-half process of surgeries and hospitalizations until he died on his graduation weekend. Our whole town stepped up to care for Daniel and his family, and it was my privilege to play a small part as an unofficial chaplain for them.

Oh yes, and all this was happening as my ministry at the church I was serving was falling apart.

I'll be the first to admit it: it was always hard for me to be a pastor in a congregation, and not just at that moment. For most of twenty-five years, I'd felt like I had little idea what I was doing or should be doing. I had few true mentors and couldn't relate to others who were considered successful in ministry. I didn't share their gregarious personalities or their comfort with the system and programs of the church. Self-righteously, I judged their theology or approach to the Bible deficient. Comparing myself to them, I realized I didn't have the ability or interest to "run a church" like they did. They were friends and fine people, but I never lost the feeling of being a square peg in ecclesiastical circles.

My twenty-five-year career as a pastor was confounded by an undercurrent of questioning, self-doubt, searching, an instinct to rebel against the conventional wisdom of my evangelical churches and their ministerial traditions and practices, and a sense of being trapped because I didn't know what else I could do. But my livelihood and the well-being of my family depended upon keeping my job. I still saw myself as a pastor, but increasingly, I didn't want to be a pastor in a congregational setting.

In early 2005, my church ministry was over. For the first time in my adult life, I had no job or prospects. I felt lost. Then a friend who worked as a hospice nurse called. Boosted by my recent experiences with Daniel and his family, I accepted a position and became "Chaplain Mike." So began a new vocational journey, one that would last for almost twenty years, serving patients and families in end-of-life settings.

I didn't realize it immediately, but at that point my true vocation and my work merged.

It may be that when we no longer know what to do
we have come to our real work,
and that when we no longer know which way to go
we have come to our real journey.

The mind that is not baffled is not employed.
The impeded stream is the one that sings.[13]

WENDELL BERRY

Since then, there have been times I've been tempted to regret I hadn't discovered chaplaincy as my life's work years earlier. However, I've learned to appreciate the journey. I know now I could never have been ready to do hospice chaplaincy work without the experiences that led me to that point.

Discovering one's true "self," which so many counselors emphasize as key to finding one's vocation, is not a simple matter. My "self" is not something static that I discover once: it develops within me and is formed over the course of my life. There may be a core self-identity I can recognize even early on. For me, that was "pastor." But it took nearly a lifetime of daily experiences to hone and clarify my understanding of that into "chaplain." Some of my pastor experiences were affirming and positive. I like to think I helped some folks as their pastor. There were also sins of omission, missteps, conflicts, doubts, and a few dead-end trails. Looking back, I thank God for mercy—for myself and for those I *mis*-pastored along the way.

I know I'm fortunate. Not everyone gets to line up their true calling with their daily work.

SOURCES

1. Garber, Steven. *Visions of Vocation: Common Grace for the Common Good.* InterVarsity Press, Kindle Edition, 2014.

2. Longenecker, Fr. Dwight. "Lent with St. Benedict: Ora et Labora, Prayer and Work" (www.ncregister.com/blog/lent-with-st-benedict-ora-et-labora-prayer-and-work).

3. Garber, Steven.

4. Askinosie, Shawn; Askinosie, Lawren. *Meaningful Work: A Quest to Do Great Business, Find Your Calling, and Feed Your Soul.* Penguin Publishing Group, Kindle Edition, 2017.

5. Askinosie, Shawn; Askinosie, Lawren.

6. Askinosie, Shawn; Askinosie, Lawren.

7. Askinosie, Shawn; Askinosie, Lawren.

8. Askinosie, Shawn; Askinosie, Lawren.

9. Veith, Gene. "The Doctrine of Vocation" (reverendluther.org/pdfs2/The-Doctrine-of-Vocation.pdf).

10. Plantinga, Cornelius. "Sin: Not the Way It's Supposed to Be" (henrycenter.tiu.edu/wp-content/uploads/2014/01/Cornelius-Plantinga_Sin.pdf).

11. Palmer, Parker.

12. Palmer, Parker.

13. Berry, Wendell. "Our Real Work," from *Standing by Words: Essays.* Counterpoint, 2011.

Little Hour Two: *Sext*

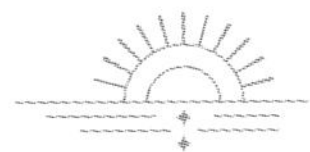

Discipline yourselves, keep alert.
Like a roaring lion your adversary
the devil prowls around,
looking for someone to devour.

1 Peter 5:8

Seek the Lord and his strength;
seek his presence continually.

Psalm 105:4

If I wanted to, I could live just barely,
refusing the gift of each day.[1]

Kathleen Norris

Craftsmanship

According to Acts 2:1–15, the Holy Spirit descended upon the early church at 9:00 in the morning, the Hour of Terce. Jesus promised this gift to empower his people to do their work of spreading the good news throughout the world (Acts 1:8). During our entire workday, through the movements of Terce, Sext, and None, we continue to rely upon divine energy to do our work.

But let's not make this overly religious. Good work also grows out of healthy lifestyle habits as well as the emotional and relational wholeness that comes from being in harmony with ourselves and others. Good work requires our entire being. It also requires an extended ability to pay attention.

I like the old-fashioned word "craftsmanship" to describe work that maintains energy, focus, and skill throughout the day. As I have observed those I consider craftspersons, I am astonished by their calm demeanor, their patience with the process, their ability to tolerate snags, complications, and their own mistakes, their flexibility and creativity to adapt to changing conditions or unforeseen obstacles, and their ability to tune out noise and distractions to keep their focus sharp. There's something about the way they work that is of a piece with nature herself and her resolute processes.

Suppose we did our work
like the snow, quietly, quietly,
leaving nothing out.[2]

WENDELL BERRY

The world watched with interest the past few years as skilled artisans, architects, and specialists from across the globe assembled in Paris to restore Notre Dame Cathedral, which was severely damaged by fire in 2019. Combining traditional methods from centuries past with modern technology, an almost miraculous resurrection of the building was achieved. The intricate skill and attention to detail, perseverance and ability to flex when needed, along with the spirit of cooperation that this took has been an inspiration.

That is complex craftsmanship on a large scale. But how about in your work? The following questions may apply to you no matter whether you are a boss, employee, self-employed worker, stay-at-home parent, student, laborer, barista, computer tech, salesperson, or retiree.

- What would it mean to you to be a craftsperson in your daily work?
- What preparation, attention, and focus does your work demand?
- What knowledge is required and how can you continue to grow in expertise?
- What skills do you need to sharpen continually?
- What kinds of cooperation and communication are needed between you and others with whom you work? How can you help encourage healthier working relationships?
- What kinds of personal growth do you need to pursue to "own" your work more fully?
- Do you know someone who exemplifies the craftsmanship you would like to emulate?

> If I am supposed to hoe a garden or make a table, then I will be obeying God if I am true to the task I am performing. To do the work carefully and well, with love and respect for the nature of my task and with due attention to its purpose, is to unite myself to God's will in my work. In this way I become His instrument. He works through me. ▪ THOMAS MERTON[3]

Fighting the demons

One barrier to doing our work well is a long-recognized condition known as *acedia*. For centuries, monks have fought this psychological-emotional-spiritual affliction, which diminishes the quality of their concentration and efforts. They call it the "noon-day demon." In the middle of the workday, when hunger growls and tedium leads to lagging concentration, workers become vulnerable to acedia.

Kathleen Norris wrote a modern classic on this malady, called *Acedia and Me: A Marriage, Monks, and a Writer's Life*:

> At its Greek root, the word acedia means the absence of care. The person afflicted by acedia refuses to care or is incapable of doing so. When life becomes too challenging and engagement with others too demanding, acedia offers a kind of spiritual morphine: you know the pain is there, yet you can't rouse yourself to give a damn.[4]

Acedia leads those in religious vocations to think prayer and good works are not worth the effort. But Norris says this condition can attack us all in our work and anything that requires focus and energy.

> Yet I have come to believe that acedia can strike anyone whose work requires self-motivation and solitude, anyone who remains married "for better for worse," anyone who is determined to stay true to a commitment that is sorely tested in everyday life.[5]

She quotes sources across the centuries who describe this demon's influence. Acedia is said to "render us slothful and immobile in the face of all the work to be done." It "signifies a state of restlessness and inability either to work or to pray." Others pinpoint a certain "bitterness of mind" that renders us cynical and indifferent, or a "boredom" that causes us to rush through our work while our minds are thinking about other things. Acedia provokes us to abhor any hint of tedium. Dante described acedia as a "black mire now to be sullen in," while Petrarch focused on the restlessness that has us constantly longing for a better situation but never finding one. Another called this a "demonic impulse and spirit of wandering."

One of the more vivid descriptions Norris quotes comes from Maria Edgeworth:

> I was afflicted with...a constant restlessness of mind and body; an aversion to the place I was in, or the thing I was doing, or rather to that which was passing before my eyes, for I was never doing any thing; I had an utter abhorrence and an incapacity of voluntary exertion. Unless roused by external stimulus, I sank into that kind of apathy, and vacancy of ideas, vulgarly known by the name of a *brown study*. If confined in a room for more than half an hour of bad weather or other contrarieties, I would pace backwards and forwards, like the restless *cavia* in his den, with a fretful, unmeaning pertinacity. I felt an insatiable longing for something new, and a childish love of locomotion.[6]

Acedia and Me offers a detailed history, analysis, and clarification of acedia in its many manifestations. It is also a personal story of Norris's own battles with this demon. She found help and comfort in the writings and practices of monasticism but acknowledges an ongoing struggle, offering no easy formula for overcoming this affliction. In one passage she does her best by summarizing monastic counsel:

> Perform the humblest of tasks with full attention and no fussing over the whys and wherefores; remember that you are susceptible, at the beginning of any new venture, to being distracted from your purpose by such things as a headache, and intense ill will toward another,

> a neurotic and potent self-doubt. To dwell in this desert and make it bloom requires that we indulge in neither guilt nor vainglorious fantasizing, but struggle to know ourselves as we are.[7]

I am heartened by the fact that Kathleen Norris has produced brilliant, lasting work that has done and will continue to do much good in the world, despite her struggles with acedia.

God willing, we may do the same.

SOURCES

1. Norris, Kathleen. *Acedia and Me: A Marriage, Monks, and a Writer's Life*. Riverhead Books, 2008.

2. Berry, Wendell. *Leavings: Poems*. Berkeley: Counterpoint, Kindle Edition, 2010.

3. Merton, Thomas. *A Book of Hours*. Notre Dame: Sorin Books, 2007.

4. Norris, Kathleen.

5. Norris, Kathleen.

6. Norris, Kathleen.

7. Norris, Kathleen.

Little Hour Three: *None*

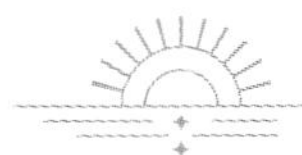

Do not lag in zeal, be ardent in spirit, serve the Lord.
Rejoice in hope, be patient in suffering, persevere in prayer.

Romans 12:11–12

So let us not grow weary in doing what is right,
for we will reap at harvest time, if we do not give up.

Galatians 6:9

Show all your faithful, Lord,
in what a full and true sense their work
follows them into your realm.[1]

Pierre Teilhard de Chardin

Ending the day

> The day is aging. Shadows lengthen as the light stretches toward evening. As the earth turns away from the sun, an ancient longing returns to my soul. It is a yearning for completion. ▪ MACRINA WIEDERKEHR[2]

When creation's work was completed each day, God pronounced it "good." Note: not "perfect" or "complete." The Hebrew word for "good" is tov. Good reverses the situation described in Genesis 1:2, when the earth is described as *tohu wabohu*—formless and empty. Note the wordplay—God took what was *tohu wabohu* and made it *tov*. God transformed a formless and empty world into one of form and fullness. The uninhabitable wasteland became a place where living things can thrive. Chaos was ordered. Wilderness became a garden. A world of potential emerged from chaos and darkness.

Theologian Jürgen Moltmann emphasizes that God is still creating. He distinguishes between God's *Original* Creation at the beginning, God's *Continuous* Creation, the "unremitting creative activity of God...that both preserves *and* innovates" the world throughout time, and God's New Creation, the goal and completion of all God's creative activity.[3]

Or, as theologian Pierre Teilhard de Chardin puts it:

> The fact is that creation has never stopped. The creative act is one huge continual gesture, drawn out over the totality of time. It is still going on; and, incessantly even if imperceptibly, the world is constantly emerging a little farther above nothingness. Through the whole breadth and depth of the cosmos, it is in truth the divine action that still molds us, as it molded the clay on the first day of creation.[4]

God's work, like ours, is never done!

The final "Little Hour," None (3:00 p.m.), transitions us to the end of the workday. As we move toward the final whistle, it is hoped that we, too, will bring our work to a place where we can say, "It is good." We will not be able to say, "It is completed" or "It is perfect." It will be enough if we can affirm our work's goodness and potential for ongoing development.

Let the favor of the Lord our God be upon us,
and prosper for us the work of our hands—
O prosper the work of our hands!

PSALM 90:17

Tikkun olam: gathering sparks

Another way to think about our work in the day's final stretch is in terms of the Jewish concept *tikkun olam*. This phrase means "to repair the world." *Tikkun olam* is rooted in a cosmological myth from Jewish tradition, told in the sixteenth century by Rabbi Isaac Luria of Safed, known as the Ari. People today think of *tikkun olam* in terms of social justice or environmental causes, but the idea is broader. Here is the story, as told by Howard Schwartz:

> At the beginning of time, God's presence filled the universe. When God decided to bring this world into being, to make room for creation, He first drew in His breath, contracting Himself. From that contraction darkness was created. And when God said, "Let there be light" (Gen. 1:3), the light that came into being filled the darkness, and ten holy vessels came forth, each filled with primordial light.

In this way God sent forth those ten vessels, like a fleet of ships, each carrying its cargo of light. Had they all arrived intact, the world would have been perfect. But the vessels were too fragile to contain such a powerful, divine light. They broke open, split asunder, and all the holy sparks were scattered like sand, like seeds, like stars. Those sparks fell everywhere, but more fell on the Holy Land than anywhere else.

That is why we were created—to gather the sparks, no matter where they are hidden. God created the world so that the descendants of Jacob could raise up the holy sparks. That is why there have been so many exiles — to release the holy sparks from the servitude of captivity. In this way the Jewish people will sift all the holy sparks from the four corners of the earth.

And when enough holy sparks have been gathered, the broken vessels will be restored, and Tikkun Olam, the repair of the world, awaited so long, will finally be complete. Therefore it should be the aim of everyone to raise these sparks from wherever they are imprisoned and to elevate them to holiness by the power of their soul.[5]

"That is why we were created—to gather the sparks." One way to evaluate our daily work is to ask, "How many sparks did I gather today?" We may not always be able to identify a positive impact we've made. However, a little reflection might reveal a contribution in which we can take joy, knowing that each spark retrieved brightens the world that much more.

Gathering a spark can signify anything that produces more goodness, kindness, and love in the world. It might be a job well done that advances the mission of one's company. It may involve making progress on a good goal. It can happen when we explore a creative solution or go above or beyond to do good.

Our dentist praises his wife, also a dentist. Over the years, they have been well matched in knowledge and ability, but he has noticed something. When she fashions a device or does a procedure, she also makes it aesthetically pleasing. She adds elegance to excellence. We may not have such special skills, but there are always ways to contribute to life's beauty.

Gathering a spark may mean making a positive contribution to one's work environment. Showing a positive spirit of initiative, drive, and devotion to craftsman-like work can lift the whole spirit of a team. Affirming a colleague's work, taking time to listen or make things right for a client, celebrating a team achievement, sitting with a struggling coworker, working through a conflict, knowing when to keep silent, thinking carefully before speaking—all these and a hundred other attitudes and actions add to the light.

Tikkun olam. We can always do more, but don't let thoughts of "never enough" keep you from recognizing the goodness of what you can contribute, even if it's just one spark gathered.

Taking moments to reflect on your work

In the next chapter we will talk about evenings, after work, as time for reflection on our day. But I also encourage you to take some moments during each day to pause and reflect upon your work.

I loved the rhythm of hospice work. Visits required my full attention and could be intense. I had to learn to be fully there each time I walked into someone's home because I never knew what I might encounter. Afterward I would leave, get in my car, and have time between visits to reflect on what I'd experienced. Sometimes I'd drive in silence, processing what I'd seen and heard, thinking about how I handled the situation, expressing gratitude, or imagining how I might have done better. After joint visits, a teammate and I would sometimes do this debriefing together.

You, too, may find opportunities during each day to pause and consider what your work is saying to you. This is especially helpful as you near the end of the day, when you can look back at what's been done, what things you've learned, and how you're feeling about the day's labors.

Remember, God paused, took a moment at the end of each day's work and said, "It is good."

It is hoped that throughout and at the end of our workday, we can too.

Remember...

A big part of each day is taken up with work. God is a worker, and humans were made to be workers too.

Two big questions in life are "Who am I?" and "What will I do in this world?" In Christian practice, these questions are addressed in baptism and teaching about vocation.

I have an overall vocation as a human being to represent God in the world, as well as vocations that I work out in various stations and seasons of my life.

People work jobs for various reasons. Finding one's "fit" may involve a journey.

The malady of acedia awaits to distract us from concentrating and doing good work.

Our work will never be "complete" or "perfect." However, we can achieve work that is "good," work that has potential for ongoing fruitfulness and that promotes tikkun olam.

Consider...

What are some of your callings? What work do you do to fulfill them?

How do you try to live out your vocation as a human being in the specific vocations where you work?

What have you learned about doing good work and battling the demons that try to undermine you?

Do you have any particular ways that you regularly reflect on your work and what it means?

SOURCES

1. K Deignan, Kathleen, CND; Osgood, Libby, CND.

2. Wiederkehr, Macrina.

3. Houtz, Wyatt. "Jürgen Moltmann on Evolution as God's Continuous Creation" (biologos.org/articles/jurgen-moltmann-on-evolution-as-gods-continuous-creation).

4. K Deignan, Kathleen, CND; Osgood, Libby, CND.

5. Schwartz, Howard. "How the Ari Created a Myth and Transformed Judaism" (tikkun.org/how-the-ari-created-a-myth-and-transformed-judaism).

Vespers

THE EVENING SACRIFICE

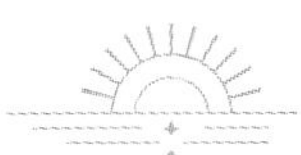

It is good to give thanks to the Lord,
to sing praises to your name, O Most High;
to declare your steadfast love in the morning,
and your faithfulness by night.

PSALM 92:1–2

Let my prayer be counted as incense before you,
and the lifting up of my hands as an evening sacrifice.

PSALM 141:2

It is time to put most of our work tools away
and turn our thoughts to making peace
with the day and with one another.

MACRINA WIEDERKEHR

Evening: a sentimental journey

I grew up in small towns in the Midwest and am unapologetically sentimental about them. Though I'm certain I would evaluate them differently at this point in my life, would wince at the flaws in their social fabric and protest the small-mindedness of their worldview, I will stubbornly cling to my provincial reveries of freedom, neighborliness, and peace that I treasure in my heart from childhood.

I loved evenings in our neighborhoods. After school and supper, I was free to play to my heart's content. With a group of friends on a ball field or basketball court, in our yard or street or in the branches of a tree, flying skyward on a swing or pedaling my bike, evenings were times for imagination and fun.

Sometimes, I played alone. With wiffleball bat in hand, I'd toss the ball up and I was at the plate in the World Series with the game depending on me. I nailed my grandfather's old catcher's mitt to the back of the garage and tried to pitch like Sandy Koufax. In the fall, I'd throw the football to myself and shake and bake my way through imaginary defenders, making first downs and touchdowns galore. In our backyard, I mowed a circle of grass short and dug a hole for golf. That lasted until a broken window or two.

In summers, neighbors walked or sat on porches conversing, drinking tea or lemonade and watching us go by on our bikes, waving and saying hi. There were trees to climb, fireflies to catch, and street games to play until dark, when parents rang bells or shouted out screen doors that it was time to come in.

Then we'd watch TV, listen to a game on the radio, or read a book until bedtime. I'd position a small AM transistor radio under my pillow through which the Monkees or the Dave Clark Five played as I drifted off to sleep. Sometimes I pulled in faraway stations from Canada that played songs unknown to me. It felt like I was being let into the secrets of a bigger, more intriguing world.

It comes back to me now in the country setting where I live when I hear a chorus of crickets resound or watch fireflies dance in the evening. As day dims, my heart becomes quiet and reflective. If I take time to walk around the yard or sit on the porch, I can let the day settle down within me.

In Marilynne Robinson's novel *Gilead*, Rev. John Ames describes a similar experience:

> "There shall yet old men and old women dwell in the streets of Jerusalem, and every man with his staff in his hand for every age. And the streets of the city shall be full of boys and girls playing in the streets thereof." That is prophecy, a vision of the prophet Zechariah. He says it will be marvelous in the eyes of the people, and so it might well be to people almost anywhere in this sad world. To play catch of an evening, to smell the river, to hear the train pass. These little towns were once the bold ramparts meant to shelter just such peace.

I'm grateful for my small-town upbringing that taught me to appreciate the evening's essence.

- The freedom to play with a heart unfettered.
- Slowing and quieting down.
- Reflecting on the day, alone or with others.

- A time to express gratitude.
- A time to find peace.

Having worked hard all their lives long
and all the long day, they came out
on the gallery down in your country,
out on the porch or doorstep in mine,
where they would sit at ease in the cool
of evening, and they would talk quietly
of what they had known, of what
they knew. In their rest and quiet talk
there was peace that was almost heavenly,
peace never to be forgotten, never
again quite to be imagined, but peace
above all else that we have longed for.

WENDELL BERRY[1]

Vespers: the evening service

Vespers (Latin for "evening") is the evening Hour of prayer. Some traditions call it "Evensong." Vespers is observed around the time of sunset or a bit later in the early evening. The Vespers service marks the transition from work to rest, day to night, light to darkness. It sets the tone for a peaceful, prayerful end of the day. In Vespers we slow down, quiet down, lay today to rest and prepare for the night to come.

Lighting candles is common in Vespers. As day darkens, glowing candles remind us that God's light still shines. Candles quiet us, softening our spirits, painting the growing night with a tranquil radiance.

Incense also plays a role in Vespers services, reflecting Psalm 141:2: "Let my prayer be counted as incense before you...." Rising incense symbolizes our prayers ascending to heaven. Its sweet fragrance is a sensory reminder of God's ever-present Spirit enveloping us in a gentle, calming embrace.

Songs of praise, gratitude, and contentment are most appropriate for Vespers, when we make a thank-offering to God for the blessings of the day. The Roman Breviary assigns hymns for Vespers that give praise for each of the six days of creation. In the evening we celebrate God's ongoing work even as we wind down our labors.

Day is done, but love unfailing dwells ever here;
Shadows fall, but hope prevailing calms ev'ry fear.
Loving Father, none forsaking,
Take our hearts, of love's own making,
Watch our sleeping, guard our waking,
Be always near.

JAMES QUINN

We may also perform our own evening rituals to move from our daytime work into evening rest and reflection. We need not attend gathered Vespers services to find evening peace. We may choose our own special candles or lamps to light, such as the clay oil lamp I bought for Gail on a recent retreat at Gethsemani. I know folks who come home in the evening and sit on the patio around a blazing firepit to wind down and recollect themselves while gazing into the dancing flames. Candles on the dinner table or throughout the house can fill our senses with light and fragrance that promote relaxation. Quiet, peaceful music may relieve tensions we've accumulated in the day's activities and interactions. An evening walk can refresh one's body, mind, and spirit. When this is done with a spouse, family member, or friend, we can share about our day, what's happening in our lives, and the future we're dreaming about.

The thief comes to steal

I know not everyone has leisure to slow down to recollect themselves in the evening hours. Our society is not built for this and hasn't been for most of my lifetime. When I read what I've written here, it sounds like I'm stuck in a bygone era. Life today is designed to steal our attention and fill our time, and that includes evenings. We can try to ignore that and forge our own path, but the winds are strong against us.

When we had children in school and extra-curricular activities, we had homework, late practices, games, concerts, and church events in the evenings. These left us coming home late, rushing everyone to bed, falling asleep exhausted, and dreading the cycle of activity restarting in a few hours. We developed some pretty awful meal habits, and it was a rare evening when we could relax together at home as a family. A long way from my childhood. From what I gather, the situation for younger families has not improved.

In my full-time job, it was not uncommon for me to bring work home to finish it in the evening, another chore that hindered unwinding and being attentive to the quieter movements of eventide. This was commonplace for members of our team, and we often complained about it. But work was relentless, and it took determination and effort to overcome the problem. To be honest, most of the time I didn't.

Television often robs me of evening mindfulness. I admit that I love to watch TV, and with streaming and binge-watching opportunities always available, it's easy to plop down on the couch and lose myself for hours in visual storyland. This is especially true in winter, when it is harder to be active and I want to hunker down and be entertained. I don't always consider this "wasted" time, because stories told well can be edifying, no matter the medium. But to be honest, I've lost a lot of time in front of the tube when I could have been attending to my body, mind, and spirit, nurturing relationships, and listening to my life.

This brings us back to the technology problem we identified earlier. It's hard to attend to God, think deeply about my day, listen to my life, have meaningful conversations with my spouse or others, or find a sense of peace and closure to my day when I'm lost inside my TV, tablet, or smartphone screen.

Writing is both biographical and aspirational. I'll be working on my evenings.

Evening: a time to be refreshed

We humans need play as much as we need work. We need to kick back as much as we need to dig in. Avocations are as necessary as vocations. In John Ames's words in *Gilead*, "to play catch of an evening, to smell the river, to hear the train pass" is as necessary to our well-being as the work we do.

My wife, Gail, is a gardener. From the onset of spring to the end of autumn, I am a "garden widower" most evenings. She relishes checking the health of her gardens, getting her hands dirty, watering, keeping ahead of the weeds and pests, and planning for the next tasks that will need attention. In winter, she's eagerly perusing seed catalogs, purchasing and organizing next season's seeds, planning garden beds. She does winter sowing in plastic jugs and keeps a steady eye on them. If I ever get around to building her a greenhouse, she'll be able to devote even more time and energy to her beloved plants.

This is not "work" for her but refreshment for her body and spirit. Evenings are prime time for her to attend to these labors of love. They bring her joy and contentment.

What refreshes you in the evening? Articles on evening self-care are pretty consistent in their advice:

- Develop an evening routine and try to maintain a consistent bedtime as its endpoint.
- Create a calming atmosphere with candles, music, warm drinks, and quiet conversation.
- Journal or spend time in intentional reflection to clear and calm your mind.
- Stay away from electronics and screens as much as possible.
- Engage in relaxing hobbies, creative activities, or quiet play.
- Take an evening walk.
- Sit outside on the porch or patio. Build a fire. Watch the sun go down.
- Pamper your body with a shower or bath, a massage, some skincare.
- Read, pray, meditate. Do some light yoga.

Invite friends to wind down the day with you. I enjoyed it when we lived in town and had a front porch where we could greet neighbors out for evening walks. (Someone once told me the world changed when people went from having front porches to backyard decks and patios.) Wendell Berry recalls the evening social habits of previous generations in his part of the world:

> After supper, when they weren't too tired, neighbors would walk across the fields to visit each other. They popped corn, my friend said, and ate apples and talked. They told each other stories. They told each other stories, as I knew myself, that they all had heard before. Sometimes they told stories about each other, about themselves, living again in their own memories and thus

> keeping their memories alive. Among the hearers of these stories were always the children. When bedtime came, the visitors lit their lanterns and went home. My friend talked about this, and thought about it, and then he said "They had everything but money."[2]

Evening can be an oasis at the end of the day to relax, refresh, and reconnect us.

Evening: a time to reflect

Macrina Wiederkehr suggests that we start the process of unwinding and reflecting on our way home from work (assuming we have some kind of a commute). If we work at home, perhaps we can take a walk or find some other bridge between our daily work and the evening.

She suggests that we ask ourselves some of the following questions after work. She calls them a "gentle assessment of [the] day." They're designed to enhance gratitude as we look back.

- What has been the greatest blessing of this day?
- What one accomplishment can I smile over?
- Is there an unfinished task that is taking away my sense of fulfillment? (If so, bless it with the promise that you will attend to it tomorrow.)
- Will I choose to relax in some way this evening?
- Am I able to look with compassion on the faces of those who have been part of my workday?
- John of the Cross says, "In the evening of life we shall be judged by love." How well have I loved this day?
- Is there anyone I need to make peace with before the day ends?

Don't think of these questions as severe self-interrogation. Don't think you have to ask or answer all of them. That's not the point. They are sample thoughts for reflection that may help us lay down the day and either leave it behind or put it in a place for safekeeping until tomorrow. "Leave work at work," as they say. Then transition into a new space, change the soundtrack, and begin the slower, quieter evening dance.

For a more intentional spiritual discipline of reflection in the evening, try the Ignatian practice of the Daily Examen.[3] Many Jesuits and other Christians participate in this end-of-day review practice.

Dennis Hamm, SJ calls the Examen "rummaging for God as we pray backwards through our day."[4] He suggests goes beyond recalling and confessing our sins, noting that our "conscience" is more than our moral awareness and judgment. It includes our entire "consciousness." The Examen helps us rummage through how we feel about everything that happened today, not just where we have fallen short.

Hamm suggests "praying backwards through the day" in five steps:

1. Pray for God's light.
2. Review the day in thanksgiving.
3. Review the feelings that surface as you review your day.
4. Choose one of those feelings (positive or negative) and pray from it.
5. Look toward tomorrow.

He emphasizes paying attention to the *feelings* that most catch our attention as we review our day. Our emotions provide strong clues that something is going on inside that we need to process. I think Hamm is right when he says that "feelings are the liveliest index to what is happening in our lives." Emotions surface first and indicate our gut response to our experiences. Until we recognize them and call them what they are, we won't be able to go further to change our thinking or habits.

Hamm's final step helps us responsibly prepare for tomorrow and then "not worry about tomorrow" (Matthew 6:34). We take a moment to address our feelings again, this time what we feel about our expectations regarding the day to come. Then we pray and leave them in God's care with the Lord's Prayer: "May your will be done on earth as in heaven."

The point of any end-of-the-day replay exercise is not to promote beating myself up or unhealthy navel-gazing. There may well be times when I look back at my day with tears and legitimate regret. I may discover that I did drop the ball, I need to ask forgiveness, I must commit to doing better. Something needs mending. However, I must also think more broadly. I face whatever the day has to teach me and come to enough peace about it so that I can lay it down and entrust it into God's care while I rest.

> When evening arrives—no matter what happened during the day, whatever *sturm und drang* occurred, whatever challenges were unmet, whatever disappointments and regrets—people have a universal desire to find a serene place where they can put all the parts of the day together in some tranquil way....[A]t Vespers we are free to let go of the day and to luxuriate in the quiet beauty of the evening. ▪ **DAVID STEINDL-RAST AND SHARON LEBELL**

Evening: a time to release

Let's talk about the importance of "letting go" or "releasing" for a moment. Not just letting go of the day but releasing what is happening inside of me as I look back.

Oliver Burkeman[5] reminds us that failing to let go can be a major pitfall. In our culture, life and work are built on the foundation of controllability. The more I can control, the happier and more "successful" I will be. But life has a way of letting us know we're not actually in charge. We need to let go of that idea.

Our emotional, spiritual, relational, and even bodily health depends on accepting limitations and learning to let go of matters outside our control. Here are a few examples of things we fail to release and some suggested talks we might have with ourselves at the end of the day about learning to let go.

I fail to let go of the idea that everything is up to me, and that if something didn't happen as planned or turn out well, it must be that I failed to put in the requisite motivated effort to make it happen.

When I reflect on my day, am I beating myself up for not working hard enough, for failing to make more happen? Am I giving myself too much credit for how much depends on me? Can I let go?

I fail to let go of being hard on myself, relentlessly driven by my inner critic. I must watch myself carefully because I can't be trusted to do good work. If left to myself, I will be lazy and self-indulgent.

When I reflect on my day, am I tempted to be unsparingly mean to myself? To think of myself in ungenerous ways that I would never think of others? To imagine that anything I did this day that was pleasurable or personally meaningful was selfish and unproductive? Can I let go?

I fail to let go of feeling responsible for other people's problems. I find it hard to distinguish between my stuff and your stuff. I fail to recognize myself as a people pleaser, thinking I'm responsible for your happiness. If you're upset with me, it's ever and always my fault.

When I reflect on my day, am I preoccupied with what others might be thinking or saying about me? Am I caught up in strategizing how I might live up to someone else's expectations or placate their disappointment in me when it might really be their problem, not mine? Can I let go?

I fail to let go of the idea that, when something unpredictable happens, it's almost always bad. I have been taught to plan well, to analyze and strategize matters carefully, to execute my life and work with firm control. I get shaken when things don't go according to plan.

When I reflect on my day, can I have peace that things have happened beyond my control? Can I distinguish between appropriate responsibility and unrealistic expectations? Can I smile at serendipity? Welcome epiphanies? Transform unpleasant surprises into good stories? Can I let go?

The last thing I want to do is make you feel like these end-of-day practices are daunting, requiring an amount of effort that subverts refreshment in the evening. But think about it: if you are preoccupied at the end of the day with unhealthy anxiety and stress, you're already working hard and finding it hard to unwind. These are not assignments, just gentle prompts you can refer to as needed. Something as simple as spending a few minutes journaling or going for a short walk might be all it takes.

I also commend "The Serenity Prayer" as a generous and simple gift we can use to release the day.

God, grant me the serenity
to accept the things I cannot change,
courage to change the things I can,
and wisdom to know the difference.

Evening: a time to recalibrate

Through refreshment, reflection, and releasing, evening enables us to reset, to retake our place in the world, with God and ourselves, with others and the life that has been given us.

In her book *Vesper Flights*, Helen Macdonald recounts a childhood evening ritual that helped her "build an imaginative sanctuary." There, she could leave behind the day's stresses and fend off fears of the night. She'd lie in bed and count the strata below her, between herself and the earth's core. Starting with the crust, she would descend through earth's upper mantle, lower mantle, and outer core until she reached its inner core. Then she would think in the other direction, naming the layers of atmosphere above her: troposphere, stratosphere, mesosphere, thermosphere, finally reaching the exosphere.

> A few miles beneath me was molten rock, a few miles above limitless dust and vacancy, and there I'd lie with the warm blanket of the troposphere over me and a red cotton duvet cover too, and the smell of tonight's dinner lingering upstairs, and downstairs the sound of my mother busy at her typewriter. ...
>
> No matter how tightly the day's bad things had gripped me, there was so much up there above me, so much below, so many places and states that were implacable, unreachable, entirely uninterested in human affairs. Listing them one by one built imaginative sanctuary between walls of unknowing knowns. ...
>
> My own private vespers felt a little like counting the steps up a flight of steep stairs. I needed to know where I was. It was a way of bringing me home.[6]

Helen Macdonald found a creative way to make peace with her day and prepare for night. Recalibrating her perspective and feelings, she found her place and felt safe in the world once again. This is a primary function of the evening time. After another day of living, we come to terms with who we are, what happened, and where we are in life. We "come home" again and reestablish a sound basis from which to start anew when the next day comes.

Macdonald specializes in writing about non-human life, particularly birds. In the chapter "Vesper Flights" in her book of the same name, she details the lives of swifts: speedy, magical birds that never touch down, "the closest things to aliens on earth." Swifts can fly for years at a time. They have nests for breeding, but they build them of things they snatch from the air as they dart about. They mate while flying; they sleep while airborne as well.

Swifts have a peculiar journey they make twice a day, at twilight and near dawn, called "vespers flights":

> And then, all at once, as if summoned by a call or a bell, they rise higher and higher until they disappear from view. These ascents are called vespers flights, or vesper flights, after the Latin vesper for evening. Vespers are evening devotional prayers, the last and most solemn of the day, and I have always thought "vesper flights" the most beautiful phrase, an ever-falling blue.[7]

Why these "vesper flights"? Scientists have learned that swifts ascend to the "convective boundary layer" above the clouds. They reach a height where they can see clearly enough to "forecast" the weather as they assess winds and weather systems. Also, at that level, they do something else that is extraordinary:

> ...migratory birds orient themselves through a complex of interacting compass mechanisms. During vesper flights, swifts have access to them all. At this panoptic height they can see the scattered patterns of the stars overhead, and at the same time they can calibrate their magnetic

> compasses, getting their bearings according to the light polarisation patterns that are strongest and clearest in twilit skies. Stars, wind, polarised light, magnetic cues, the distant rubble of clouds a hundred miles out, clear cold air, and below them the hush of a world tilting towards sleep or waking towards dawn. What they are doing is flying so high they can work out exactly where they are, to know what they should do next. They're quietly, perfectly, orienting themselves.[8]

Recalibrating. The swifts teach us that evening is the perfect time to "quietly, perfectly, orient" ourselves once more. To do so, they leave one space and enter another, where they can see clearly and sense creation's vibrations that help them reset their lives for what comes next.

So may we.

Remember...

Evening marks the transition from work to rest, day to night, light to darkness.

In the evening Vespers service, candles, incense, songs, and prayers of gratitude and contentment are used to encourage a peaceful and prayerful end to the day.

There are many habits and distractions that can steal mindfulness and rest from us in the evening.

Evening is a time to be refreshed, to reflect, to release, and to recalibrate.

Consider...

What is your evening routine like at this point in time? Were there other times or settings in your life when it was more relaxing, reflective, and restorative?

What hinders you from having those kinds of evenings now?

Do you engage in any particular practices to help you end the day well?

SOURCES

1. Berry, Wendell. "A Letter to Ernest J. Gaines," from *Leavings: Poems*. Berkeley: Counterpoint, 2010.

2. Berry, Wendell. "The Work of Local Culture," from *What Are People For? Essays by Wendell Berry*. Berkeley: Counterpoint, 1990/2010.

3. "The Daily Examen" (ignatianspirituality.com/ignatian-prayer/the-examen).

4. Dennis Hamm, SJ. "Rummaging for God: Praying Backwards through Your Day" (ignatianspirituality.com/ignatian-prayer/the-examen/rummaging-for-god-praying-backward-through-your-day/).

5. Burkeman Oliver. *Meditations for Mortals: Four Weeks to Embrace Your Limitations and Make Time for What Counts*. New York: Farrar, Strauss, and Giroux, Kindle Edition, 2024.

6. Macdonald, Helen. *Vesper Flights*. Grove Atlantic, Kindle Edition, 2020.

7. Macdonald, Helen.

8. Macdonald, Helen.

Compline

RECEIVING THE GIFT OF REST

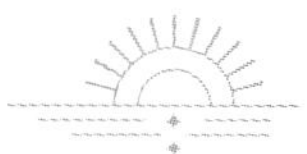

Return, O my soul, to your rest,
for the Lord has dealt bountifully with you.

PSALM 116:7

I will both lie down and sleep in peace;
for you alone, O Lord, make me lie down in safety.

PSALM 4:8

It makes all the difference in the world how we fall asleep.

DAVID STEINDL-RAST AND SHARON LEBELL

Saying goodnight

It is an act of faith to fall sleep at night. We pass, willingly, into an unconscious state for hours, trusting that the world will go on without us, that we'll be safe until morning, that we'll awaken to a new day.

Compline is the final Divine Hour prayed each day in Christian traditions. It prepares individuals and the community for bedtime, called "The Great Silence"—the dark stillness of night. In Compline we say goodnight to God, ourselves, the day, and each other. In an act of profound trust, we lay our bodies and spirits down and enter another world of dreams and repose.

Those who pray Compline ask for God's presence and protection when they are asleep and unaware of potential dangers. As David Steindl-Rast and Sharon Lebell remind us:

> The characteristic psalm for Compline is the one in which we put ourselves into the shelter of God's protecting love. As wayfarers surprised by the night might look for shelter in trees somewhere or in caves, so we go under the "wings of the Most High."

The service for Compline is brief, held in darkness or candlelight, quiet and sweet in its imagery of God's loving embrace and care.

O holy Lord, we pray to thee,
throughout the night our guardian be;
in thee vouchsafe us to repose,
all peaceful till the night shall close.
Christe, qui, splendor et dies

In *Prayer as Night Falls: Experiencing Compline*, Kenneth Peterson, singer in a Compline Choir at St. Mark's Cathedral in Seattle, Washington, outlines Compline's history and development in Christian tradition and the revival of interest in praying the Divine Hours that started in the 1950s and '60s.

Peterson notes that "The story of Compline begins before history itself, in the feelings and responses engendered by the transition from day to night."[1] It has roots in both Jewish tradition and in rituals practiced by other ancient cultures. Compline had its Christian beginnings in the fourth and fifth centuries through St. Basil and John Cassian; it became an official part of monastery life in the sixth century.

A typical Compline (or Night Prayer) service consists of:

- An invocation
- Examination of conscience, confession, and absolution
- Hymns, psalms, and Scripture readings
- A Gospel canticle
- A prayer and blessing
- A song to Mary

Compline is my favorite service at Gethsemani Abbey, perhaps because am a night person, with a "lunar spirituality," as Barbara Brown Taylor calls it. The service is so peaceful, the atmosphere serene, the spirit generous and sweet. I exhale a deep sigh, release the day's tension, and transition to the place of rest.

The most consoling part of Compline for me is when the sanctuary goes dark except for candles illuminating an icon of the Virgin Mary. The monks then sing a beautiful hymn to her. Nothing in my Protestant evangelical background could have prepared me for how moving this is.

On my first pilgrimage to Gethsemani, I pondered why this resonated so deeply with me, and I realized that there was an entire *feminine* ethos missing from my tradition's spirituality. The faith I knew was masculine and hard-edged, with nothing like the gentle mother's touch that is experienced when God's children offer devotion to Mary. It is like being tucked into bed by the tender hands of your mother, feeling her kiss on your cheek, basking in her love. Of course this should be a part of my faith! What child with a caring mother would not want to say a tender goodnight to the Mother of God at end of day?

At Gethsemani, an invitation to come forward to receive a blessing from the abbot follows the Marian hymn. He blesses us, splashing us with holy water to symbolize our cleansing before bedtime. We go to bed washed, blessed, and secure in God's love, ready for a good sleep.

It has been said that the prayer Jesus prayed on the cross, "Father, into your hands I commend my spirit," was taught by Jewish mothers to their children as a bedtime prayer. Likewise, on our beds we lay the coming night, our life, our future, and even our death into the hands of our loving God.

Protect us, Lord, as we stay awake;
watch over us as we sleep,
that awake, we may keep watch with Christ,
and asleep, rest in his peace. Amen.

May we all find ways of falling asleep with this trusting, peace-filled spirit at the end of each day.

Remember...

It is an act of faith to fall asleep at night, to trust in God's protection and care.

At bedtime, we say goodnight to God, ourselves, the day, and each other.

Consider...

How is it for you, falling asleep at night?

SOURCES

1. Peterson, Kenneth V. *Prayer as Night Falls: Experiencing Compline*. The Paraclete Press, Kindle Edition, 2013.

Reprise: I hope you'll dance...

Here are two summary lists to which you can refer as you dance with creation, living mindfully through the hours of each day. May you go in peace, know God's strength and blessing in all you do, and play your part in repairing the world just a little bit each day.

Living Daily through the Hours

In the night watches we befriend the darkness.

At dawn we watch for God's new mercies.

Going to work, we remember our calling.

In our labors, we pursue craftsmanship and fight temptation.

Late in the day, we try to bring our work
to where we can say, "It is good."

In the evening, we are refreshed, we reflect, we recalibrate.

As we go to bed, we commend ourselves
into the care of a loving God.

Scriptures for meditation through the Hours

IN THE NIGHT

I think of you on my bed,
and meditate on you in the watches of the night.
Psalm 63:6

IN EARLY MORNING

The steadfast love of the Lord never ceases,
his mercies never come to an end;
they are new every morning;
great is your faithfulness.
Lamentations 3:22–23

AT THE BEGINNING OF THE WORKDAY

He has told you, O mortal, what is good;
and what does the Lord require of you
but to do justice, and to love kindness,
and to walk humbly with your God?
Micah 6:8

IN THE MIDDLE OF THE WORKDAY

Let the favor of the Lord our God be upon us,
and prosper for us the work of our hands—
O prosper the work of our hands!
Psalm 90:17

LATE IN THE WORKDAY

So let us not grow weary in doing what is right,
for we will reap at harvest time, if we do not give up.
Galatians 6:9

IN THE EVENING

Let my prayer be counted as incense before you,
and the lifting up of my hands as an evening sacrifice.
Psalm 141:2

AT BEDTIME

I will both lie down and sleep in peace;
for you alone, O Lord, make me lie down in safety.
Psalm 4:8

EVERY DAY

Surely goodness and mercy shall follow me
all the days of my life.
Psalm 23:6